"*He's OK, She's OK* is a down-to-earth book about men, women, and the struggles that arise from their natural differences. Easy to understand and filled with good, sound, practical advice, it is a 'must read' for anyone interested in understanding gender styles and improving their love relationships."

John C. Robinson, Ph.D.
Author of *Death of a Hero, Birth of the Soul*

"This engaging and useful volume can help both men and women by increasing their understanding of each other's motives and modes of communication."

Edward Zigler, Ph.D.
Sterling Professor of Psychology, Yale University

"The compactness of this wise, witty volume belies its power. The authors' solid experience and theory offer practical exercises and advice to help couples weather the unpredictable storms those differences can produce. Priority reading for people interested in true partnership."

Nina Boyd Krebs, Ed.D.
Author of *Changing Woman, Changing Work*

"The skills and instructions of Jeannette Lofas have helped to change my life. This book can do the same for others. I enthusiastically recommend it."

Linda Lavin
Actress

"An important work for men and women to understand and deal with the problems they have had for so long in understanding and in communicating."

Arline Caldwell, M.D.
National President
American Society of Psychoanalytic Physicians, 1993-1994

"Gender differences has become the popular topic of discussion in the nineties. This book will help you welcome and enjoy those differences and have fun talking about whether you can identify with them. Instead of using differences to separate the sexes and make them adversaries, this book will help you to embrace the differences and make you accepting, supportive partners."

Elva Anson, MFCC

HE'S OK

Honoring The Differences Between Men and Women

SHE'S OK

Jeannette Lofas, CSW
Joan MacMillan, MSC, MFCC

Tzedakah Publications
Sacramento, California

He's OK She's OK: Honoring The Differences Between Men and Women

Manufactured in the United States of America

Cover and text design by Comstock's Design & Litho,
Mary Burroughs, Creative Director and Jill Raymond.
Cartoon illustrations by David Moore

For information, address
Tzedakah Publications
P.O. Box 221097
Sacramento, CA 95822
1-800-316-1824

Lofas, Jeannette.
He's ok, she's ok: honoring the differences between men and women / by Jeannette Lofas and Joan MacMillan.
p. cm.
ISBN 0-929999-11-8 : $12.95
1. Sex roles. 2. Sex differences (Psychology) 3. Communication – Sex differences. 4. Man-woman relationships.
I. MacMillan, Joan. 1938-. II. Title.
HQ1075.L63 1995 94-48409
306.7 -- dc20 CIP

12 11 10 9 8 7 6 5 4 3 2 1
First Edition

TABLE OF CONTENTS

DEDICATION

To our clients who constantly urged us to write this book.

To Bob who taught us what "real" men do and do not do.

To Dave who loyally read, assisted and graciously supported this work.

Liz — Thank you for the next generation's perspective.

To the men and women who already know and to those who will learn to honor their differences.

ACKNOWLEDGMENTS

Michael Gorman, our editor, who honed this work with his insights and editorial excellence.

Tony Ferrante who elegantly coordinated all the many aspects of making this book work.

David Cawthorn for Tzedakah's work toward healing the world. Thank you David for your vision.

Mary Burroughs, Comstock Design & Litho, for a great book design.

INTRODUCTION

The Line & The Circle

Once upon a time there was a Line and a Circle,
And Line was strong and thick and powerful, and going.
And Circle was a pool, warm and wet, and waiting.
Circle said to Line, "What's wrong with you?
You always go straight, never looking to the right or the left.
Being a line must be very boring."
Line said to Circle, "What's wrong with you? You go nowhere,
You have no direction. You go 'round and 'round.
You never go anywhere, except back to where you began."

He's OK, She's OK explores biological differences which are substantiated by scientific facts. It is different from other books which focus on male/female characteristics and relationships. It is about the architecture of man and woman. Our intent is to honor the mysteries and celebrate the differences — just the way we are. This book is not about all men and women, but about the majority of men and women.

For many years we have heralded the concept of being "color blind," not realizing that the attempts to make us color blind are based on the belief that we are too limited to handle the rich variety of colors which make up society. Perhaps, the same holds true for "gender blindness."

As a way of making the material in the book more accessible and more practical, we have included quizzes throughout. Use these to check your own attitudes against the information provided in the chapters. Give yourself permission to personalize the discussion of gender; all of us do anyway. Here is a preliminary quiz to get things started.

STOP

Check out your notions of men and women. Look to "Quiz Answers And Explanations" in the back of the book for explanations and interpretations of the quiz.

Instructions: These exercises will allow you to gauge your "masculine" and "feminine" attributes and your attitudes about those attributes.

As you enjoy working, remember that no one is completely "masculine" or "feminine." In fact, if you're "normal," you'll find that on many items you will test differently from what is typical of your gender. Relax. That's what makes it fun, complicated, and interesting.

Save your results and refer to them as you read *He's Ok, She's Ok.* This will give you a personal connection to the information which will help you learn about you and yours.

I am:

_______ Male   _______Female

QUIZ 1 — GETTING STARTED

A. Looking at Differences

Instructions: In the spaces provided, write down the number which best reflects your ideas and feelings about the following statements.

1 = Strongly agree
2 = Somewhat agree
3 = Undecided
4 = Somewhat disagree
5 = Strongly disagree

1. _____ Except for a few features of plumbing, men and women are pretty much the same.

2. _____ Men and women are very different physically, but that's all.

3. _____ Men and women only do things differently because of the way they're brought up.

4. _____ There is absolutely no physical reason for homosexuality. It is all psychological or learned behavior.

5. _____ The feminist movement celebrates the glory of woman and of feminine values.

6. _____ Homemaking is an important career.

7. _____ We wouldn't have nearly as many problems in our male/female relationships if we understood our differences and celebrated them.

8. _____ Men act more quickly upon a problem they can solve than do women.

9. _____ Women talk about feelings with more ease than most men do. Women may tend to "talk it through" before they act.

10. _____ I know how to deal with gender problems in my life.

B. Your Dealings With Gender

Instructions: In what areas do you have the most problems with the opposite sex? When you are done, look to the back of the book for answers and implications. But first, rate the following areas according to the scale below:

1 = Poor
2 = Fair
3 = Good
4 = Excellent

1. _____ Affection

2. _____ Children

3. _____ Communication

4. _____ Control

5. _____ Criticism

6. _____ Disciplining the children

7. _____ Making decisions

8. _____ Money

9. _____ Not knowing why they do what they do

10. _____ Sex

11. _____ Stepchildren

12. _____ Other

About your partner:
Rate your overall communication with him/her.

13. _____ Poor

14. _____ Fair

15. _____ Good

16. _____ Excellent

Rate his/her overall communication with you.

17. _____ Poor

18. _____ Fair

19. _____ Good

20. _____ Excellent

Overall, rate your compatibility with him/her.

21. _____ Poor

22. _____ Fair

23. _____ Good

24. _____ Excellent

CHAPTER 1

Where Gender Touches Down: The Results of Not Knowing

A quick glance at the newsstand confirms what most of us already know all too well — gender plays a significant role in many of the problems in our lives that we care about most. Magazine after magazine carries articles exploring the male and female spin on these — dating, marriage, parenting, self-esteem, work, social order.

Because gender is such an integral part of every aspect of our lives, we cannot escape the gender impact on social problems. Yet, despite the almost universal acknowledgement that gender plays a role, little agreement exists on what that role is or how specifically it influences us.

The first step in answering that conundrum is looking at the way gender intrudes itself into issues that preoccupy us as a society.

The Breakdown of the Family

The ideal family of the past worked like a well-managed business. Each person had a role to fulfill. Each role provided a necessary element in the success of the whole group. Most often those roles were established along lines of gender.

Today, however, as males and females, we expect things of each other which our ancestors would never have expected. Our gender role models have changed or ceased to exist. We now ask men to do housework and women to work all day long outside the home. When a typical couple comes home, he's tired and often doesn't want to talk as much as she does, and she feels the need to share what went on in her day as well as her feelings about it. Weekends bring questions of who does the cleaning, the yard work, the shopping, and other homemaking tasks. Who earns more money, and does that person have the right to do fewer tasks at home? Who is supposed to take care of the kids? Every day brings questions of who is doing more than the other.

Our positions in the family have become fuzzy. As social and economic forces have worked to dismantle the traditional roles, the family as social institution has begun to break down. With no clear substitute for the "old way," we are now faced with a divorce epidemic.

Judith Wallerstein, Ph.D., in her book *Second Chances* (Tickor and Fields, NY, 1989), in a ten to fifteen year study of middle and upper class children of divorce, details the effects on children of divorce:

- Only 45% of children do well after divorce.
- 41% are worried, underachieving, self-deprecating, and often angry.
- In the year following divorce, women with childen average a 73% drop in their standard of living, while their husbands average a 42% rise.
- 40% of the nineteen to twenty-three-year-old young men had no goals, a limited education, and a sense of having no control in their lives.
- 33% of the girls between nineteen and twenty-three, who previously seemed to be unimpaired by the divorce, suffered what was labeled as the "sleeper effect." As soon as they experienced their first serious relationship, they left it — for fear it would not work out.
- 60% of children felt rejection by one of their parents — usually the father.
- 50% saw their mother or father undergo a second divorce.
- 50% of the divorced women and 30% of the men were still intensely angry at their former spouses.
- Too often, divorced parents are chronically disorganized, unable to meet parenting challenges, and often lean heavily on the child.
- The children of divorce tended to do well if mothers and fathers, regardless of remarriage, resumed parenting roles,

putting differences aside, and allowing the children continuing relationships with both parents. Only a few children had these advantages.

- Most children of divorce felt the lack of a template, a working model, for a loving relationship between a man and a woman.

The result of these trends is fertile ground for the eventual demise of the family. And what of the old saying, "As goes the family, so goes the society?"

John and Mary Divorced and Didn't Know Why

Central to the issue of family breakdown is the splitting of marriage relationships. The fifty to sixty percent breakups stagger us. There are few places where our identities as men and women play as central a role as in our intimate, committed relationships. The interplay of male and female, self and other, is truly intricate. Yet in our daily counseling with couples, we are amazed by the simplicity of the accepted responses to, "Why did you divorce?"

He:
It didn't work out.
We fell out of love.
She said I wouldn't talk to her.
We fought.

She:
After we got married, he lost interest in me.
He wouldn't talk to me, listen to me, or look at me.
He either shut down or bullied me.
He couldn't be affectionate without wanting sex.

Many of us simply do not know the causes of our breakups, nor what to do about the resulting chaos in the family and in society. Our inability to find the roots of the problem too often leaves our men and women without partners, our homes without families, and our children without the adequate training in how to be productive and civil citizens.

It was funny in the movies, but children left to feed and care for themselves many hours a day is not funny in reality. The juvenile crime statistics rarely prompt a good belly laugh. Children who are left to their own devices do fill their time, but without adult supervision and guidance, they too often fill time in ways which are not good for them or for others.

"Home base," the safe place to raise the kids where adults meet physical needs and model for the children, for the most part — is gone. Once, the woman was queen of the home. Extended families lived close by and provided support for her work. Homemaking was an integral part of the social structure. Today, mothers and fathers both work outside the home, though children are still expected to live there. Even the word *homemaker* is no longer respected.

Joan used to call herself "Holly Homemaker." In 1960, she began her career teaching Homemaking in public schools. Until recently, she was embarrassed about her many years teaching "just homemaking."

We seem to have devalued the creation of this safe home base, this place where we are nurtured and can grow strong with respect for self and for others. Devalued are these things:

- the place where the man interacts regularly with children to demonstrate the ways of the work place, the hierarchy, the rules of the game and how to "get the job done — now!"
- the place where the woman interacts regularly with children to provide modeling, manners, mores, social values, and ethics. The place where she provides the central role of relationships in human happiness.

Self-Esteem

A strong sense of self is integral to a productive and happy life. It is the foundation of all the relationships we build. Gender plays a key role in our discovery and acceptance of ourselves and in our bridging the gap between ourselves and others.

We interact and contribute to life in accordance with our belief systems about ourselves. Much of that sense of self is formed by age five. Those first five years are spent watching and listening to Mom, Dad, and other significant adults. Very young children don't yet question, but naturally believe, all their parents say to and about them. If children hear they are welcome and worth caring about, and that there is an expectation that they are good and capable, that becomes their belief system about themselves. If children hear they are in the way or not important enough for parents to spend time with them to model and teach values, skills, and boundaries, the result is a lack of self-respect and respect for others, and that becomes their belief system.

Children learn by example. Little girls watch and emulate Mommy. Little boys walk in Daddy's steps, doing what Daddy does and treating others the way they see Daddy treat others. Both boys and girls learn how to be in relationship with the other sex by watching Mommy's and Daddy's relationship, played out daily in the home.

The Future

Many of us do not know what to do about the chaos in the family and in the society. Yet our children are not being shown how to be male and female and productive and civil. Children, without a positive home and good care during the parents' working days, become children without self-esteem or esteem for others, without accountability, ambition, or direction.

It is clear that the lack of roles play a tremendous part in much that ails our society. But at what point is gender an issue worth addressing in the battle to better our lives? Is gender a hitchhiker on the vehicle of divorce and juvenile crime and family breakup? Or is gender the driver of these problems?

These questions can have no answers until we examine how we understand gender, personally and as a culture.

CHAPTER 2

Characteristics - The Man's Way and The Woman's Way

QUIZ 2

Instructions: Respond with the number which best suits you. Work quickly and do not compare with your partner until you have finished. Do not make your partner "wrong." Go for the insight. Have fun!

Look to the back of the book for answers and concepts.

Do you or are you:

1 = Always
2 = Usually
3 = Sometimes
4 = Seldom
5 = Never

Differences and Development

1. _____ read road maps easily?

2. _____ task-oriented?

3. _____ people-oriented?

4. _____ like to work on one task at a time, until it's finished?

5. _____ enjoy talking and sharing about a problem?

6. _____ focus singly on the solution to a problem?

7. _____ intuitive?

8. _____ like to work with numbers?

9. _____ like to shop?

10. _____ judge distances easily and accurately?
(Montagu, Ashley, The Natural Superiority of Women, New and Revised Edition, Collier Books, MacMillan Publishing Co. NY, NY, 1992)

Take a minute to compare your results with your partner's. Now compare them to the chart below which we believe describes the typical male and female responses. The characteristics we present apply only to most, not all, men and women. We are describing general male and female attributes, not absolutes.

There are innumerable exceptions.

He:	**She:**
Follows his anatomy. Like the line and the phallus, he moves forward in one direction.	Follows her anatomy. Like the womb she is circular, bringing people to her, surrounding herself with things and people.
Focuses on achieving his goals.	Focuses on affiliating with others.
Pays attention to how things are put together, and how they are working. Is driven by the need to know and to fix.	Innately pays attention to the relativity of children, family, and society. Is driven by the need to relate and create.

Penetrates the snarling traffic to achieve his goal, never stopping, never asking directions. The goal is always there, like the prey in his ancestor's mind.

To him, asking for directions means he is the lower ranking male.

Meanders, looking into store windows. She notices the coat on that woman, the children of another, and the luscious new cherries in the supermarket.

Like her foraging ancestors, she looks and differentiates. Her radar is on; her attention circling, sorting, and investigating.

Although most of us easily spot the differences between males and females, we often don't admit to our observations for fear of sounding sexist or old-fashioned. We think perhaps our conclusions are a result of a cultural bias. We distrust our own ability to see. Yet the perceptions seem valid. Are there, in fact, biological reasons for the differences we observe?

Brain Differences

The Male

During the first few weeks in the uterus, all human fetuses are essentially the same. Then, six weeks after conception, the male fetus receives a massive bath of testosterone, and the male brain is forever changed.

(Moir, Anne Ph.D. and David Jessel, BrainSex, Bantam Doubleday Dell Publishing Group, Inc. NY, NY, 1989)

The effect of the male hormonal brain-bath is to narrow the corpus callosum, which is the switching mechanism between the left and right hemispheres of the brain. Thus, the male brain architecture is, to a large extent, the source of the task-oriented, one-thing-at-a-time, unilateral, focused thinking that we associate with the male way of being. He is linear, and so communicates in a linear way — A, B, C. You are wrong if you miss D.

The Female

In the female fetus, the corpus callosum remains constant and considerably wider than in the male. This wider passageway allows greater transmission of data between the brain hemispheres. Not only can she process left brain logic, but she also has easy access to the right brain: seat of intuition, emotions, and imagination.

Her bilateral thinking allows her a special skill in knowing the relatedness of people and things. She is less linear, and more circular in her thinking. She may jump from A to B to L, driving most men crazy. Her circular communication is difficult for the male brain to process.

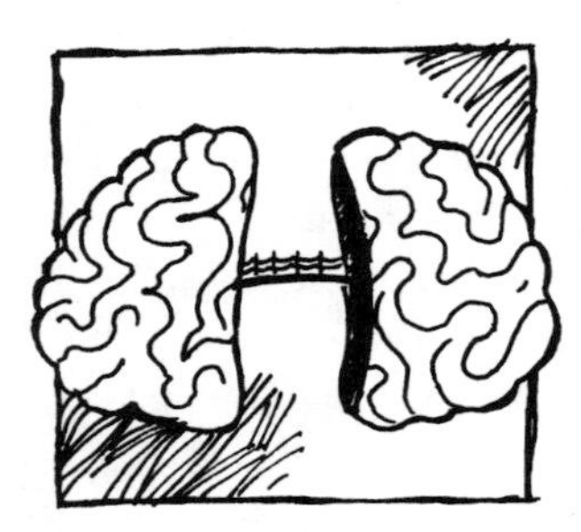

He:
Deals with the linear, the sequential, the concrete, and the logical. The male thinks objectively, looking at outside data, lining them up, one thing after another to get an objective, bottom line answer.

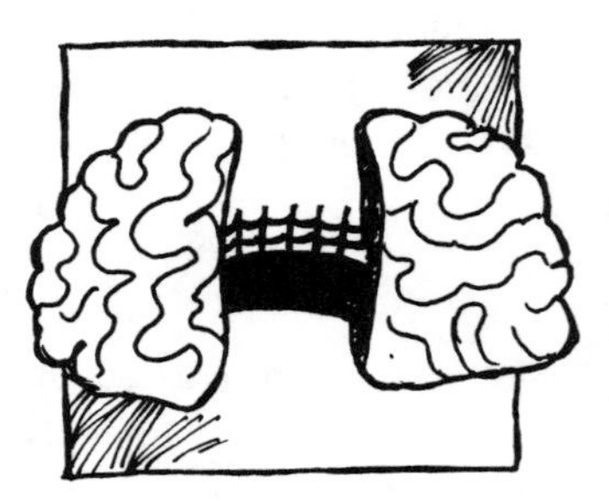

She:
Thinks with both sides of her brain — the left linear, the right intuitive and feelings. The female switches back and forth. She is primarily a subjective thinker, looking inside for answers as to how she feels, and how things relate to her and her world.

He:
Thinks in a linear manner like a calculator: 1 + 1 = 2.

She:
Thinks more like a radar system, scanning and receiving data, relating back and forth, up and down and around like a circle.

Babies

Baby Boy and Girl Twins Show us the Dissimilarities

Fran and Jim Johnston had been through it all. They had been married more than 10 years, all the while trying to conceive a child. They finally consulted with a fertility expert which resulted in the birth of twins — a boy, Stephen, and a girl, Sally. Believing that every person, regardless of sex, could do anything, Fran and Jim agreed to raise the babies with no sexual stereotyping.

Within days of taking the children home from the hospital, both Fran and Jim noticed the differences. Baby Stephen spent hours watching the crib "bumpers," cloths of different textures and colors, while baby Sally spent most of her time sleeping. When she was awake and being held, Sally would gaze in the direction of her parents' faces as they talked to her. She would be very still and express obvious pleasure in the tender touches of her parents. When Stephen was being held, after a short time, his eyes would wander in the direction of other sounds.

Studies have verified the Johnston's observations. From birth, girls are more sensitive to touch than are boys, and are less tolerant of noise, pain, and discomfort. Boy babies are more wakeful, and show more interest in objects and in sounds other than the human voice. Repeated research shows that from the earliest years, girls talk more than boys.

It Continues in Nursery School — Girls Relate, Boys Relate and Push

In linguistic studies of nursery school boys and girls, 100 percent of the girls' noises were relationship noises through conversation and language. Only 68 percent of the boys' noises were relationship directed. The remaining 32 percent reflected male themes of pushing, shoving, and jostling each other. The noises sounded like, "brrr," "bam," and "bang."

(Kohn, Robert, "Patterns of Hemisphere Specialization in Preschoolers," Neuro Psychologia, Vol. 12)

When She Starts to Tell Him What to Do — The Four-Year-Old's Tea Party

A little girl asks a little boy to have a tea party with her. She shows him to a little table with carefully set toy tea cups. He reluctantly obeys, putting down his truck, picking the tea cup.

She says, "Let's pretend I am the Mommy, you are the Daddy. Do you want cream or lemon?

Sugar? Two lumps or one? No, take your tea cup and hold it like this, not like that."

The boy looks perplexed and uncomfortable. The little girl instructs, "Now pass me the cakes."

The little boy reaches down, grabs his truck and hits her with it.

Girls can be directive like little Mommies. Already, in this tea party story, we see how little boys and little girls do not communicate by the same criteria. For boys, taking orders is innately and subconsciously a sign of low ranking. This little boy, driven by his inherent nature, evened the score.

Girls: Allure, Charm, and Affiliate

Talking all the while, little girls dress up, wear Mom's clothes and put on her makeup. They model themselves after their mothers, practicing what Mom does. They play and talk, using the arts of being alluring, inviting, and charming.

Jerree Levy, professor of psychology at the University of Chicago, has spent twenty years studying the human brain. She writes of being astounded watching her own fifteen-month-old daughter at a party in her home:

"My daughter . . . dressed in her teeny little nightie . . . came into the room . . . with this saucy little walk, cocking her head, blinking her eyes, especially at the men. You never saw such flirtation in your life."

Little girls seldom shove or vie for position by pushing or jostling. Girls charm, smile, play, flirt, invite, reject. Little girls ask by suggesting, "How about we play tree house?"

Boys: Try to Direct Each Other

Boys communicate with each other by directing, "Come over here. Throw me that ball." They learn from older men. Boys do what men do. Men often communicate with silent signals — signals that women do not know. With boys and men there may be little talking, just doing.

Eight-Year-Old Boys and Girls Play By Different Rules

Boys are playing a game out in the fields. They have a dispute over the rules. There is a heated discussion, almost a fight, with lots of shouting and pushing. Then the boys make up new rules and continue the game.

Girls are out playing. There is a fight over the rules, and they continue to fight. They cannot resolve the fight. The girls pick up their dollies, and go home. The game is over.

Most little girls, trained by their mothers with the ritual or ceremony around relationship activities, like to do it "the way you are supposed to." And they direct each other to that end. Their interest in roles and rules has to do with affiliation, not hierarchy.

He Would Be What He Would Be

The writer H. H. Monro "Saki" wrote a telling story about a liberal household where the couple sought to suppress their son's natural male aggression by refusing him a set of tin soldiers. Instead, they supplied a set of tin civil servants and teachers. They felt that all was going well until one day they went into the playroom and saw that he had set out a royal battle between regiments of toy teachers and model bureaucrats. His parents, fortunately for the child, realized he would be what he would be.

(Moir, Anne, Ph.D. and David Jessel, BrainSex, pp. 7, 8)

The differences are inherent. We are designed that way. On the "nature vs. nurture" debate, we know that it is the "nature" of the male and female to be dissimilar.

To Illustrate: Homosexuality — Physiologically Determined?

This point of innate differences is made even more powerfully by the recent studies on homosexuality. These studies provide evidence which shows that homosexuality may well be physiologically dictated and not a life style choice.

(Henry, William A. III, "Born Gay?", Time Magazine, July 26, 1993)

Male homosexuals tested positively for marked hormonal differences from heterosexual males. One study shows an area in the brain (the suprachiasmatic nucleus) which scientists say determines sexual orientation, to be nearly twice as large in homosexual men as in heterosexual men. Tests on lesbians are beginning to show a higher level of male hormones.

In September 1993, the journal *Science* cited a study that gay men reported a higher percentage of homosexual male relatives than found in the rest of the population. Intriguingly, almost all of the relatives were on the mother's side of the family. It is now thought that homosexuality may be carried through the mother.

On the other hand, articles in January and February, 1994, *Harvard Mental Health Letter* argue that studies showing physiological causes of sexual orientation are "weak."

Arguments included:

- Studies were done with subjects recruited through advertisements in gay-and lesbian-oriented publications.
- Brain dissections showing a larger connection between the right brain and the left brain, as in the female, were performed on subjects who died of AIDS. This could possibly account for the differences found.

In essence, the *Harvard Mental Health Letter* articles embrace the old supposition that the roots of homosexuality are solely psychological rather than a combination of physiological and social factors.

We disagree. Despite the objections, no contemporary studies on homosexuality support a purely social or psychological causation. All of the recent studies indicate a strong genetic component.

Tragically, many young homosexuals are still sent to therapists to "cure" their sexual orientation. The resulting horror stories are the antithesis of responsible, modern therapy. Until 1974, The American Psychiatric Association listed homosexuality as a "mental disorder." However, the only homosexuals studied to that point were those with problems who came seeking psychological help. Because the conclusions fit the cultural bias of the time, no one bothered to ask if there were healthy, well-adjusted homosexuals living peacefully in the community. Once someone did, and studies found there were indeed healthy homosexuals, the APA took homosexuality off its list of disorders.

Just as early understanding of the genetic roots of homosexuality was clouded by cultural prejudices and social assumptions, so, too, our understanding of biologically based gender differences is too often hindered by the same forces. We conclude that given our natural, genetic diversity, it is time to recognize, understand, respect, and honor our differences. Once we move beyond our fear of diversity, our study of gender differences can become fascinating and rewarding. Let's now look at some of those differences.

CHAPTER 3

THE DIFFERENCES

"All conflicts between people and all wars between nations are from not respecting our differences."
Sathya Sai Baba, Indian Guru

The Forgotten Wisdom of Lines and Circles
The essences were known
of Lines and Circles
of the hunter/warrior and the gather/nurturer.
Men, follow their line
and go in the direction it points.
Women circle
people and things around them.
They seem to go in no direction,
and in all directions at once.
One time, long ago,
the Line and the Circle
they were proud of each other.
She was honored
for her mastery of the mysteries of the circular
of relationships, people, and things.
He was honored
for his mastery of power and straightness
of solutions, conquests, and tasks.

Sorting Systems: How We Organize our Realities

Most males and females differ in the way they organize the world. Therefore, we value things in dissimilar ways.

Most Males Want:	**Most Females Want:**
a job to be done	a relationship to people and things
a solution to the problem	empathy for the person with the problem
a chance for victory	an opportunity to relate
to focus on one thing at a time	to see many aspects of a thing
to say, "I shot a deer!"	to say, "You shot Bambi!"
independence	intimacy
a group, a team	a best friend
to dominate	to connect
his rank	her link

How We Are Different

There are many exceptions to this portrait of men and women. We are creating a broad, generalized template here. These characteristics are typical, but by no means universal or exclusive. Yet when we learn the norm, we can enjoy the exceptions even more.

The Male

"Frogs and Snails and Puppy Dog Tails:" The Nature of Boys

In a healthy world, little boys naturally play King of the Mountain. Boys push, throw, and shove to ascertain relative strength and dominance. Naturally selected over the centuries for the hunt and protection, they have inbred in them a determination to discover who is the leader and who plays what role in the hierarchy. Boys' verbalizations reflect this. The way they relate is partly designed to find out who is the best at what.

Boys compete. Competition is fierce, but generally not personal. If one boy wins at arm wrestling, the other boys compliment him and say he is the best arm wrestler in the neighborhood, and "He is my friend." Here then is their connection, "I am the friend of the best arm wrestler, but I am the best basketball player, and our other friend John is the best at soccer." The boys, from early on, order themselves in a hierarchy of talents, strengths, and abilities.

Men are organized to determine these rankings with each other, and most of it is below the level of consciousness. It is the normal way that men relate to each other, and it feels right. There is pleasure in this muscling and bantering, this "puffing out."

In male animals, bold coloring and the ability to appear larger or puffed out have served to attract females and satisfy the ongoing quest for the dominant male and for the survival of the species.

In groups of male animals, we seldom see a democracy but rather an organization based on a hierarchy of ranking in the group. Innately, the male animal competes with other males. From early on, boy monkeys constantly wrestle and play-fight with each other.

Hunter/Warrior — From Youth to Adulthood

In addition to determining status and dominion, this male jostling and pushing prepares boys for the role of the hunter/warrior. The hunter/warrior goes out and captures the prey or another warrior's land. The male is also organized to defend boundaries. He stands guard when other warriors challenge his turf. The warrior protects his family's, his tribe's, and his nation's boundaries.

Note that these seemingly primitive qualities are reflected in contemporary male behavior. Males achieve status by giving orders and by using insistence. Therefore, most males are not organized to listen well. For the male, intent listening and looking directly at the other is a sign of subservient status. Instead, men "rib" each other and joke for status. Males interrupt to show interest and status. They are doers and oriented to fix problems. Emotional problems which cannot be fixed or solved may either be ignored or challenged. The male tendency is to consider feelings a sign of weakness and vulnerability. So, they are hesitant to share their internal thoughts.

In general, males are more comfortable speaking with several people than with one person where personal issues can be the topic. All this was formulated at a subconscious level over centuries, and continues to determine characteristic male patterns of communication today.

The Hierarchy Once Established, Men Build a Tight Team

Men who work with their hands, who move things, and use their brawn clearly reflect the male hierarchy. We see it in construction workers. They have coffee. Their conversation often centers on playful mental one-upsmanship and sometimes friendly physical pushing. Once they find the hierarchy, the leadership, and the pecking order, they become a tight team and perform well in groups to obtain dominance over something else — whether it is a stag, a skyscraper, or a corporation. On Wall Street, the game of male hierarchy and dominance is still evident, but it is played with different tools. They wrestle with companies and money, but the same primal, innate form remains constant.

The Coffee Shop

We see this in coffee shops. Male construction workers sit at one table and talk about "it." Their "it" is what is going on outside, in their environment — what they are doing about it, and what other men are doing about it, who did it better, and what group won.

Male energy is about the world "out there." Their talk seems superficial to women, but males connect with each other this way. Working together they form a male camaraderie. To help each other, they alter the OUTSIDE environment. When one is sick, they assist in a "male" way. "I'll take some of your load." His pal does something to make his work easier. Should something come up which is emotionally uncomfortable, men may change the subject to something more manageable. "How about those Broncos?"

Sitting at another table at the coffee shop is a regular group of female friends. One isn't feeling well. Her friends help her to feel better. "What can I get you? I have pills in my purse. Try some yogurt. Have some hot soup." The women can't wait to get something INSIDE of her. "How does it feel now?"

The Female

"Sugar and Spice and Everything Nice:" The Nature of Girls

Little girls are naturally full of words. Remember, 100 percent of the sounds made by the little girls in the nursery schools were about relationship. Because of the female's right brain/left brain thinking — her ability to switch between the linear event, intuition and feelings — she is able to be a master at negotiating relationships and reading character.

Nurturer/Gatherer - From Youth to Adulthood

A girl's ability to recognize and distinguish between details comes from her ancient heritage as a "gatherer." Her way of functioning has always been to ask: "Is this face different? Is it friendly? Trustworthy? How is this item different from that? Do I want it or need this or that? Now? In the future? In the past?" Her way of being is not about hierarchy, but about socialization, relativity, and the gathering of things and people.

Competition Between Females

Competition between girls can be fierce, divisive, and also hazardous. When girls fight they often leave or exclude each other. When jealousy or distress arises concerning one girl, the others want her "gone." Females have no compelling reason to reconcile with their rivals. To the contrary, getting rid of another female increases the chances in the continuing female competition to win the strongest and most powerful male who will take the best care of her and their babies. Females do not hunt or war together, so there is little reason for them to form a team which must function to solve disputes.

Corporate Gender

The male thrusting together toward a goal may well allow groups of men to be more achieving than groups of women. Women, being more relationship-oriented, may focus more on relating to each other than on the task or goal to be achieved. One might speculate that this is one of the reasons women find it harder to work within the male norms of business. This does not mean, however, that the male approach is somehow better.

Businesses would do well to realize that there are lessons to be learned from the female perspective. Often, in fact, what is missing in the major companies is the woman's point of view in doing business. In addition to focusing on the linear, she may have greater intuition regarding the character of people doing business with the company. In addition, many women use their feminine abilities to think forward and backward and sideways remembering countless details, coming up with surprisingly important decision-making information.

Women who start and run their own businesses often achieve great success. These women use what is currently being called "horizontal management techniques." The work is done in cooperative work circles with workers on an equal level of responsibility and reward rather than on a level of a hierarchy. Management is in the feminine mode.

Businesses need to see an integration of the best of the male and the female modes of management to compete in today's world.

Let's look at some of the pertinent gender characteristics that arise from the hunter/gatherer dichotomy:

HE
The Task

Wants to know the task and complete it.

Wants to compete alone or with his buddies until winning. "Goes for" anything.

SHE
The Relationship

Wants to know, or may intuit, the relationship between individuals and things.

Wants to come together as a group and talk about it before she decides.

He Highly Values:

Being praised for his tasks.

Not being criticized.

Being trusted.

Not being told what to do.

Being appreciated for the bounty he gives her.

She Highly Values:

Being appreciated for what she does.

Being listened to, without him telling her the answer to problems.

Feeling loved.

Talking about what to do.

Feeling appreciated for her care taking.

He Takes Offense When:	**She Takes Offense When:**
She tells him what to do.	He continues to drive not asking directions, even though they will be late.
She continues to switch topics.	He is so damned linear.
She continues to chatter about a topic when he "got it" and is mulling it over.	He gets quiet, thinking about the topic, without saying anything.
She says she is shopping for one thing and comes home with another.	He is reluctant to go shopping with her.
She seems to be "self-centered," and talks so much.	He refuses to talk or listen and "stonewalls" her, leaving her out.

To Succeed

A Man

Must pit himself against an image he has of success. Every time he attempts something, he must re-evaluate and attempt again, constantly putting his ego on the line and often being humbled by the results.

A Woman

Must move through male-structured worlds. She must learn to compartmentalize, and must learn to put up personal boundaries.

Status

He	She
Often, initial conversations are to create status and to establish the hierarchy. Who is one up? Who is one down?	Often, language is used to create a relationship. Do I like you? Do you like me?
Gives orders and makes them stick.	Belongs, compromises and gives in.
Boasts.	Understates her achievements to be accepted by the male and by the female.
Practices hierarchy in playtime.	Play is overtly more equal, less hierarchical. Vies for leadership in more covert ways.
Giving praise in a hierarchy is done only by the one who is "one up."	Giving praise is part of nurturing.

The integration of the female mode into business can be seen in our own working experiences:

Gathering the News, Jeannette:

As a reporter, working exclusively with men, I began to know that often they did not see an event the way I did. "Gathering the news," I began to realize that men and I covered a story very differently. In local television news, a classic story is the coverage of a fire.

When the men covered a fire story, the tradition was to go to the burning building and film the reporter standing in front of it, saying something like, "Here on 70th and Main we are at a twenty story building, valued at approximatly value 50 million dollars. So far, two firemen have been hospitalized and four occupants have been found dead."

I would film the fire story differently. For example, we would film the burning building, but open with a tight shot of a fireman carrying an old lady down a ladder from the fire, lovingly, big and gentle, sweet and strong. We would see her face and the fireman's face. I would narrate. "Mrs. Land had lived here for 20 years. She is a grandmother of six and is well-known for her chocolate chip cookies."

My stories were most often about relationships. I gathered the news in terms of people, while the men most often looked at the story in terms of facts and logic; how much, how tall, how many.

When the news director saw my first fire story, it was already on the air. After the piece, he came and looked at me, lambasting, "What was that? You are making this into human interest, soft news. We do hard news here!"

The next day, the boss heard from the station owner's wife that she liked the piece and liked me. So he called me into his office, saying, "Well, whatever the hell you are doing out there — we'll just go do it!"

Six Women Therapists, Joan:

Joan's counseling center in suburban Sacramento is owned and directed by six women therapists. This all-female management has created problems. When the partners are faced with issues involving property management, budget, intern supervision, roof leakage and the like, they talk about it. How will each decision affect the people involved? Will the arrangement be inconvenient for each renter? Will it diminish the ambiance of the center? Every decision is about community and the comfort of all the players.

Male renters often ask if they can use the center's group room without the usual fee, "just this time," and "because of this good reason." This is business. Men compete for the best deal. Women renters simply pay their fees, determined amounts, all the while engaging in pleasant conversations with one of the partners — enjoying the community.

The partners appreciate the warm atmosphere of the Center, known throughout the state. They realize this was built because of "kinder, gentler (feminine) stuff." But they also wish for quicker and tighter (more masculine) business procedures.

Bob and Jeannette in the Film Business. She "Gathered." He "Hunted."

I "gathered" the film project: book, proposal, people, and directors. When it came time for "making the deal," my husband "cut" the deal. He, as the director of the film company, would cast out their directors, put in ours, chop down percentages, and battle them down on money. I would go to the bathroom and cry.

He would follow me into the lady's room. He would take me by the shoulders. He would take out his handkerchief and blot my tears and say, "What the hell are you whimpering about? It is just business!"

"But I spent hours talking to all those people! And you're upsetting them and hurting them. You're acting like a brute! You're beating them up!" I whimpered.

"Hey, this is business, darling! Just business. You had better get used to it!" he would reply.

And indeed I had to. That was the way the business was run. My tears were not going to change the bottom line.

What was in this for me? I became "realistic" about my expectations. Males did business this way.

Taking Positive Advantage of the Differences

In the field of law enforcement, we see the usefulness of these differences. The female police officer is often good at calming the angry suspect and using her intuition to uncover their relationship to others in question. The male police officer, on the other hand, may be better at the chase; at hunting down the offenders. Police departments all over the country are beginning to take advantage of different male/female skills.

QUIZ 3 — KNOWING THE DIFFERENCES

Instructions: Work quickly and do not compare until both have finished. Have fun and enjoy your differences. Check yourself in the back of the book.

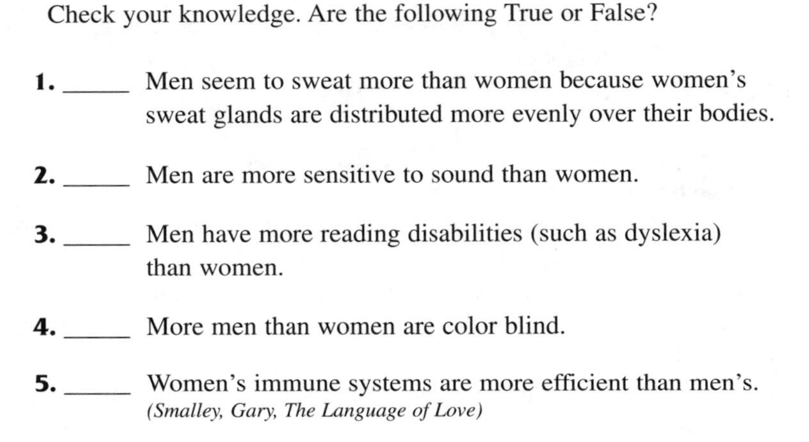

Check your knowledge. Are the following True or False?

1. _____ Men seem to sweat more than women because women's sweat glands are distributed more evenly over their bodies.

2. _____ Men are more sensitive to sound than women.

3. _____ Men have more reading disabilities (such as dyslexia) than women.

4. _____ More men than women are color blind.

5. _____ Women's immune systems are more efficient than men's.
(Smalley, Gary, The Language of Love)

It is clear that in both physical and mental characteristics, nature has made men and women very different. In the next few chapters, we will be exploring the ways that these differences manifest themselves in our daily activities. We'll look at such things as work, play, parenting, and love.

CHAPTER 4

Work and Play

QUIZ 4 — WORK AND PLAY

Instructions: Work from hunches. Do not stop and think. Do not compare until you have both finished. Celebrate your differences. Look in the back of the book for more information on this exercise.

Do you:

1 = Always
2 = Usually
3 = Sometimes
4 = Seldom
5 = Never

Work and Play

1. _____ enjoy thrilling action movies with explicit sex, violence, and physical prowess?

2. _____ enjoy having several things going at a time?

3. _____ base self-value on where in the hierarchy you are in work outside the home?

4. _____ take sometimes dangerous risks in work and play?

5. _____ plan ahead, to be safe in work and play?

6. _____ like to be in charge of a business meeting?

7. _____ like to be in charge of a party?

8. _____ enjoy hotel stays?

9. _____ simply glance at a restaurant bill and pay your approximate share?

10. _____ receive a restaurant bill, note what you had and spend time negotiating your share?

Line and Circle Opened a Store

One fine day Line and Circle opened a business together.
And Circle was always going around and around
talking to people.
And Line was always hunting new things for the store.
And the people liked what Line discovered,
and liked coming into the store and talking to Circle.
The store was a great success.

Coming Home

He:

When he comes home from work, he has spoken his 12,000 words for the day. "He already gave at the office." He's out.

That he held his own with that bastard in accounting was important. But how he feels about it won't change a damned thing, so he chooses not to talk about it.

She:

The things she saw and subtleties she notices and what she felt are important, and she still has some of her 25,000 words for the day when she gets home.

The way someone acted toward her was important to her and she wants to talk about it and how she feels. Often, he won't talk and she feels lonely.

The Way We Carry Our Necessities

Has the barest necessities in a small dull brown or black wallet — money, credit card, license. His world is out there, no need for more.

Carries in the circle of pocket book all variety of things — bags inside bags, money, keys, combs, little books, bigger books, brushes, and makeup, pencils, paper, and more. Her world is within, and with her.

Takes care of the outside.

Takes care of the inside.

Work

Defines himself by what he does, what he gets, and his rank among other workers.

Defines herself by who likes her, who she knows, how she feels, and now also by what she does and gets.

Shopping

Goes into the store looking for London Fog raincoat, 42 long. They don't have it. He leaves.

Goes to the store looking for blouses. She finds some, doesn't buy any, and foraging, ends up in the furniture department.

Sports

Wants to see the other warriors.

Is not interested unless she knows somebody.

Risk-Taking

Is socialized and trained throughout life to take risks.

Often, does not know how to risk. Is not as socialized to take risks.

Sports, sex, and business reinforce taking risks and learning from failures.

With success defined in this way, many females simply will not play.

Babe Ruth was the
Home Run King.
He also struck out the most.
In relationships with the female, the man learns that he must ask many times before he hears one yes.

Does not get the practice a man does when dating. She can, but does not, have to ask him out and risk rejection.

With sex he learns that there will be no sex if he takes no risks. "There are about 150 opportunities for rejection for the male from first eye contact to first intercourse."

The more attractive, the less she has to risk rejections. Has less experience putting her ego "on the line" in risk taking.

The result is he takes rejection less personally.

Can tolerate less failure. Takes rejection personally.

For eons has been organized to risk rejection with the female.

Is organized to tease, invite, and select the best male to mate and father her young.

Socially

Needs more space in every sense. Stand further apart from each other, lean back further in chairs. They look straight ahead while talking.

Can be physically closer to others. Women talk face to face.

Misses social nuances when assessing others.

Better judges character.

Abstract.

Intuitive.

CHAPTER 5

How We Communicate

Malese and Femalese, the Languages of the Line and the Circle

QUIZ 5: HOW YOU COMMUNICATE

Instructions: Note the number which best suits you.

Do you or are you:

1 = Always
2 = Usually
3 = Sometimes
4 = Seldom
5 = Never

Section A — About You:

1. _____ like to chat with friends on the telephone?

2. _____ have a best friend?

3. _____ speak with ease in business meetings?

4. _____ make social telephone calls easily?

5. _____ hesitate to ask for directions when lost?

6. _____ speak authoritatively enough so people listen to your opinions?

7. _____ give compliments easily?

8. _____ say a thing once and be done with it?

9. _____ cry easily?

10. _____ display anger easily?

11. _____ think it is rude to interrupt?

12. _____ maintain eye contact in a conversation?

13. _____ explain details of how something works?

14. _____ talk readily about your accomplishments?

Section B — Couple Relationship:

15. _____ enjoy tests which gauge the quality of a relationship?

16. _____ work to enhance a relationship?

17. _____ bring a gift or flowers to a significant other?

18. _____ feel responsible to call to "make a date?"

Compare your answers with ours at the end of the book. If you took this quiz with your partner, take a minute to discuss your answers.

Trying to Communicate as Lines and Circles

The Circle was talking to her friend Oval.
She said this, and then they did that,
and on the way there, they chatted and sat.
The Circle was talking to the Line.
She stopped. "You are not listening.
You ask me and then you don't listen,
and now look at the way you are looking."
The Circle rolled her eyes,
"I am not doing anything," said the Line.
"What is the point of your story?"
He directed, tapping impatiently.
"You are going round and round. My head is spinning."
The Circle snapped back. "You always ask, 'What is the point?'"
"Yes!" the Line struck back, red with anger.
The Circle was now moist with tears
and she spun away, saying again and again,
"You don't love me. You don't love me."
And they went to bed without talking.

Female Communication

She Talks to Connect and to Clarify

Females engage in self-disclosure and tell stories about themselves and others to build relationships. They sort things out by talking, clarifying to themselves and to others just what is in their minds. They repeat stories, giving many details. Females listen long and well, interrupting only to elicit more information. A woman's face expresses connection with the speaker. She faces him or her, maintaining eye contact.

To signal to the male that she is not a threat, she nods in agreement and often lowers her head and looks up, cocking her head to one side. This demonstrates she places herself in a non-threatening mode to the male. If she tells him what to do, this may indicate to him she is placing herself in a hierarchical position above him. He may fight or flee.

Most often women understate their accomplishments. They may do this for several reasons, not the least of which is to try not to threaten the male's rank. Nor do they want to infringe on the other person's sense of self-worth.

With A Male She Signals He is One-up

Taxi Drivers and My Beloved Bob

As a television and radio reporter, Jeannette had New York City press license plates on her car for sixteen years. As a result, she knows the timing of most of the traffic lights in New York and how to get around the city in the fastest possible way.

Bob absolutely hates it when Jeannette tells male cab drivers what to do. "Take West End to 66th and then cross over. Do not go by Lincoln Center at this hour." Bob cringes. "The guy knows his business. Do not tell him what to do," he will chastise.

Once Jeannette asked the cab driver where he was from and how long he was in this country. He said he was "from Russia and here for a month already, and making good money."

Lately, she has gotten into the cab and said nothing. Why should they have a ruined evening just because Bob tries to preserve the manliness of the cab driver from the prods and directions Jeannette gives? So she develops a plan A and a plan B. If they miss the first movie because they are delayed in traffic, Jeannette has a plan for a second movie about thirty minutes later.

It works well. Bob takes care of the guys and Jeannette stays quiet. Does she want to be right, or have the power of creating a fun evening? After all, Bob can't help it. This stuff has been in his genes for 30,000 years.

A Woman Wants to Hear That He Cares

A woman needs to hear expressions of love and concern. Relationship becomes real to her when it is verbalized. It is not enough to silently assume that love is there, as men often do. Men speak when there is a problem to be solved; otherwise they rest content that the love that was in place yesterday is still in place today. Because women talk of their feelings, on the other hand, silence is not reassuring, but rather, threatening. She wants, and tends to give, verbal confirmation.

Male Communication

Most men in groups have a heightened sensitivity to hierarchy, the "ordering" which begins early in childhood. The order is established by who is stronger, faster, bigger. This ranking is done subconsciously. It continues in the classroom, and grown men continue the hierarchy on the job and in sports and leisure activities with other men. Because of their comfort level with this structure, men communicate more readily at work and at sports than at home.

A man processes internally, and speaks only when his point of view is ready to state — once. When he converses, his interest is often shown by interrupting, challenging, and stating his points of view.

Since this is not the woman's style, she may think he is discounting her. Our female clients often express anger that their men "always" disagree with what they say.

Men grow tired of talking more quickly than women do. Intricate conversation is harder for them. They speak about a task and solutions to the task. To a man, a woman may seem to have no end of words or the need to speak them. For the man, words are the means to an end. If they don't go anywhere, what's the point?

Men Communicate with Silent Signals to Each Other

Men communicate facing outward and toward the "hunt" or the "battle field." Much of their communication is done with silent signals still used today — ways often not understood by women. In a restaurant, a man holds up a hand to say, "I'll get this one." The other men understand. Men look at their children with a "that's enough of that" look, and the children stop what they were doing.

The Psychiatrist and his Lady: Owen & Alexandra

Owen is a psychiatrist. He is tall, handsome, quick, friendly, and sometimes ill-tempered. His wife Alexandra is lovely — blond, womanly, and elegant as a hostess. She has a quick and sharp tongue; she is witty and sometimes sassy. A few months into their marriage they came to see me.

Alexandra said, "He doesn't listen, he doesn't understand. He was wonderful before we got married — attentive and caring. What happened to my man?" Alexandra was uncomfortable and angry. She shifted in her seat and looked at me. Owen was losing all patience with her talking about what he should and shouldn't do. I could see his eyes glaze over. I could see his mind leave the room as Alexandra went through a litany of complaints about him.

As I listened to them I began to notice all the hallmarks of gender related problems. He stopped listening to her as she got more and more into her feelings — the right side of her brain. She described her pain with him — just like current thinking said to do. She discussed the event, the feelings it aroused, what he did, what she did, and what others said.

I stopped her.

First, I talked to Owen. We discussed his opinions about the latest findings in psychiatry: Prozac, issues with insurance, data, facts. Owen seemed to perk up, and we had a good discussion together — linear to linear, task to task, event to event, solution to solution.

After a while I said to him, "Now listen to how I talk to Alexandra."

I then began to talk to Alexandra about my new rug, the weather, new movies, the newest fashions, did she want more coffee, and then about the rug again.

I noticed that as I spoke to each one, the other one focused away and grew bored and annoyed. And then I told them what I had just done. With Alexandra, I had talked the way women talk. With Owen, I had talked the way men talk. "Now, Alexandra," I said, "what did Owen and I talk about?"

"Oh, you know, medicines and boring stuff," she said.

"And Owen? What did Alexandra and I talk about?"

"The rug," he said. He said after the rug and the movies, he hadn't been listening hard enough to notice anything else.

I had videotaped the session. We watched it together. We took note of Owen's face as Alexandra and I talked. We saw on the video that when she noticed him scowling, her response was to talk faster and increase the tempo of the talk. Using the film, I showed Alexandra how she had lost Owen. He wasn't following her circular mode of thought.

I showed Owen how he had given up on the conversation and how he had stopped listening. I told him that most males were unable and unwilling to follow the circuitous route of female communication.

It is abundantly clear to me that Owen and Alexandra had a classic problem of men and women. They do not speak the same language.

It took only a few more sessions to teach these two intelligent people their different modes of talking. Owen learned to put some relationship talk into his conversations about work, and Alexandra learned that if she wanted to get a point across to Owen she had better stick to one topic at a time. With her lady friends she could talk in a circular mode, but not with Owen. As well, Owen learned that his colleagues were glad to hear about his linear deeds, but Alexandra was not.

The Way We Speak

He:

68% of noises from a little boy are conversational. The other 32% are noises, pushing, and shoving — bam, brrrr, rumm.

Speaks 12,500 words a day.

Talks later.

She:

100% of noises made by a little girl between the ages of two and four are conversational and about relationships.

Speaks 25,000 words a day

Uses sentences earlier, and uses more words in sentences.

Conversation

He:

Talks about one issue at a time, going for a solution.

Likes to have a focus for conversation.

Asks longer questions, making clear just what it is he wants to know.

Speaks more readily to more than one person.

She:

Begins speaking about one thing and brings up other things.

Is comfortable with no plan.

Listens, waiting to understand by hearing the rest of the story.

Speaks more readily in private, one to one.

Problem Solving

Listens to a problem and offers a solution. If she goes on and on, not giving him topics he can fix or solve, he may not listen at all.

Listens to a problem believing the speaker will sort out a solution while talking it through, as females do.

Creates a ten-point plan in his head, and alone.

Gives sympathy, "Aw, poor baby." She just listens.

Avoids verbal conflict with a female. Fears being pushed into powerless right brain feeling mode.

Considers verbal back and forth as a part of communication.

May not respond if he suspects a verbal barrage from her.

"Talking it out is how we sort it out, darling," she says.

May withdraw or get angry.

Gets upset.

Listens best when issue is told in story form.

Listens well to fragments, filling in details in her mind.

Conflict

Uses insistence to win. May be aggressive or stoically silent.

Seeks to mitigate conflict. Can fight dirty, use blackmail, or endlessly lobby to win her point. Or may leave.

To present opposite points of view shows interest.

To present opposite points of view means one is arguing.

Sharing Concerns

Is irritated by her wish for him to share concerns.

Great desire to share concerns.

Males and Females Misinterpret Each Other's Non-Verbal Communication

A man walks into the house. He is quiet and looks angry. She asks him what is wrong. He says, "Nothing." Remember, a man does not naturally "burden" the woman with problems he is having. This man is upset at a driver who cut him off. He chooses to say nothing about this to his wife until he cools off.

What does she assume? Most often, that he is angry with her. Defensive, she reacts to perceived criticism and retaliates. He becomes aggressive or disappears. The argument begins.

CHAPTER 6

Love

QUIZ 6: LOVE

Instructions: Respond as best suits you.

Do you:

1 = Always
2 = Usually
3 = Sometimes
4 = Seldom
5 = Never

1. _____ volunteer to say "I love you" to your partner often?

2. _____ think to say, "I love you" to your partner?

3. _____ work long hours at your job as a way of expressing love for your mate?

4. _____ emotionally support your partner's work?

5. _____ do things to show partner your love?

6. _____ show love by asking to talk with your partner?

Love

The male says, "I told you I loved you six months ago. Why do you keep asking?" She says, "You never tell me that you love me."

There are male characteristics of loving, and female characteristics of loving, and as with so many things about gender they are different, a fact acknowledged by experts in the field.

John Gray, author of the popular book *Men are from Mars, Women are from Venus* (Harper Collins, 1992), says:

"The enormous task of figuring out what our partner needs is simplified, greatly through understanding these twelve different kinds of love . . ."

Scott Peck in *The Road Less Traveled* says that love isn't a feeling. Romantic love begins as a feeling. In romantic love we are delightfully confused about each other's boundaries: "I don't know where you begin and I end." Peck says that mature love is wanting the highest good for the other. Love is what we do for our partners in seeking their highest good.

Given the inherent differences in the ways men and women approach love, and given the degree of trouble in contemporary relationships, we say emphatically that we must work. The romantic beginnings of a relationship happen spontaneously, but in order to transform that beginning into a fulfilling relationship, yes, we must work, work to define and then nurture the love between us.

Partnership

In loving one another, we must build a partnership. In partnerships, the talents and assets of the various partners aren't the same.

"Tom" and "Bob" were Wall Street businessmen. Bob was the up-front man. He had all the words and could sell anybody. He never had the numbers exactly right, and he didn't care. You never saw him without Tom. Tom did not talk. He was so quiet one could think of him as boring. But Tom had all the numbers, names, and data in his head. It was together that Tom and Bob could sell the biggest deals. Both were brilliant — Bob as a deal-maker/salesman, and Tom as a numbers man. Neither blamed the other for his inadequacies. They made wonderful use of their abilities. They were a perfect partnership.

Making A Partner Wrong Does Not Work in Partnership

It is as partners that we discover the genius in each of us, and seek our partner's and our own highest good. In a loving partnership one does not make the partner wrong. If we do, we not only make the partner wrong, we make ourselves wrong and the whole relationship wrong. Such scapegoating does not work! We can agree to disagree, but not to "make wrong."

In male/female partnerships, we have a lot to learn about each other. It is important to listen so we can learn how men and women love differently. In that way, we avoid judging our partners by our own gender mode, thus making them wrong.

John Gray in *Men are From Mars, Women are From Venus*, (Harper Collins, 1992) goes on to say:

"Women need to receive	**Men need to receive**
1. Caring	1. Trust
2. Understanding	2. Acceptance
3. Respect	3. Appreciation
4. Devotion	4. Admiration
5. Validation	5. Approval
6. Reassurance	6. Encouragement"

A Man Needs to Feel Good About Himself to Love

He does not want to be made "better." He did not like corrections from his mother when he was a child, and does not like them from his lady now. He sees corrections, no matter how lovingly given, as accusations that he is doing something wrong. He balks. He may run. He may fight. Or, he may make the change. He may feel like a good little boy, or a well-adjusted male.

However, disapproval, lack of acceptance or praise for what he has done, turns him off from loving and even from sex. What he wants to know is that she will accept him and love him anyway, complete with his hunter/warrior ways.

A Woman Needs to Feel That He Cares About Her to Love

A woman needs to feel that he cares about her, her thoughts, her concerns, their children. She needs to feel that he understands her and respects her — the way she is. She needs not to feel put down for her feelings, no matter how silly he thinks they are. She needs to feel safe with him. Does he know how important certain things are to her? Will he simply accept that she likes to shop and to talk on the phone?

John Gray describes six common mistakes men and women make with each other when attempting to express love:

"Mistakes women commonly make

1. She tries to improve his behavior or help him by offering unsolicited advice.
2. She tries to change or control his behavior by sharing her upset or negative feelings.
3. She doesn't acknowledge what he does for her but complains about what he has not done.
4. She corrects his behavior and tells him what to do, as if he were a child.
5. She expresses her upset feelings indirectly with rhetorical questions like, "How could you do that?"
6. When he makes decisions or takes initiatives, she corrects or criticizes him."

"Mistakes men commonly make

1. He doesn't listen, gets easily distracted, doesn't ask interested or concerned questions.
2. He takes her feelings literally and corrects her. He thinks she is asking for solutions so he gives advice.
3. He listens but then gets angry and blames her for upsetting him or for bringing him down.
4. He minimizes the importance of her feelings and needs. He makes children or work more important.
5. When she is upset, he explains why he is right and why she should not be upset.
6. After listening, he says nothing or just walks away."

Independence

He

Thinks silently, alone in his car, or in his cave.

Knows what he thinks by mulling it over in his head, alone.

Intimacy

She

Speaks her thoughts in order to know what she thinks or feels.

Knows what she thinks as she hears herself talking about it.

Listening

He	She
Feels listening is subordinate.	To listen is to learn and simply means to listen.
Responds less.	Makes many responses and comments.
Interrupts to clarify or correct the speaker, which means he is interested.	Uses fewer interruptions.
Interrupts to establish dominance.	Interrupts to signal understanding.

Wants to know "How high is it? How far? How many are there? What is the task?"

Shifts back and forth between "How many are there? Do I know them? Are they good people? Does this feel right? How far is it?"

Says it once, expects results.

Says it again and again if she gets no response. He calls this nagging. This repeated "asking" may sound like "Mother," and he may close down.

Tends to speak in flatter tones of voice.

Often speaks in a variety of high steady and low tones.

CHAPTER 7

Sex

QUIZ 7: SEX

Do you or are you:

1 = Always
2 = Usually
3 = Sometimes
4 = Seldom
5 = Never

1. _____ consider yourself sexy?

2. _____ consider yourself to be a "stud?"

3. _____ have multiple orgasms more easily than your partner?

4. _____ turned on by the way your partner looks?

5. _____ aroused by looking at a stranger of the opposite sex?

6. _____ aroused slowly, by someone you trust?

7. _____ wish to have sex often with different partners?

8. _____ wish to have sex only with someone you love?

9. _____ fall asleep after having sex?

10. _____ get annoyed if your partner falls asleep after having sex?

11. _____ believe foreplay is something you must do to please your partner?

12. _____ experience foreplay as necessary for you to enjoy sex?

13. _____ fear you will lose your desire if your partner goes too slowly?

Few things arouse our frustrations with gender differences like sex. However, sex can also elicit our profound wonder and enjoyment of those same differences. A little understanding can decrease the frustration and increase the enjoyment. With that in mind, let's take a look at some of the male/female differences that affect this most potent area of our lives.

Sex and the Tricks of Nature

He:
Performs like a microwave.

After orgasm, a hormone is released which causes him to fall asleep.

Has millions of seeds and looks for a nice warm place to put them.

Wants to have sex often.

She:
Is like a crock pot.

After orgasm, a hormone is released which causes her to be wide awake.

Has one egg monthly and looks for the best and strongest hunter/father.

Wants to have sex often with the man she loves.

Is turned on by what he sees.	Is turned on by what he says, what he does, and what he touches slowly.
Wants to get up, get in, and get off.	Wants a thousand years of foreplay.
Wants to do it with no hands.	Wants a man with slow hands.

Beyond the droll trickery of nature, there is a serious side to honoring differences in sex. Since the beginning of history, the phallus and the vulva have been depicted as sacred and sex has been approached as a magical mystery. There is a power in the union of these differences, power that can give much to us if we honor it.

What Assurance Does a Woman Want?

1. That he cares for her, that she is not an object with a nice warm place for his penis.
2. That he cares enough to learn how to make love to her.
3. That he won't expect "Wham bang thank you, Ma'am."
4. That he doesn't study his car manuals more than he studies manuals about how to sexually please a woman.
5. That he knows how women work in general; that a man is more like a pressure cooker and she is more like a crock pot. She "cooks" more slowly.

6. That he looks at foreplay as an art form and that it starts at the beginning of the evening — at the restaurant. That foreplay includes a sense of play — teasing with whispers in her ear and with his touch.

7. That he remembers her body and what pleases her specifically.

8. That birth control has been agreed upon and handled in advance.

9. That he is disciplined and manages his ejaculation and doesn't come too soon. No "Whoops! I'm sorry," without protection, especially during the fertile part of her cycle.

10. That he listens for her moans and groans and sighs of pleasure when his hands, mouth, and body are turning her on.

Orgasm

John Gray says that her orgasm should come before his. We agree. It is only polite. However, we believe that his use of the word "orgasm" is incorrect. Change that word to "orgasms." Many women are capable of having multiple orgasms.

The male needs to know her capacity and endeavor to satisfy it. The male usually can have only one orgasm, unless he is young, or hotly in love, or it is early in the relationship. To keep her happy, he makes love with her to provide her with as many orgasms as possible.

The Clitoris

Women often talk with each other about a man's lack of skill with the female body: "He is so bungling. Half the time he cannot find it. He is not even on it. He was working away like it was as big as his penis!"

Women seldom have vaginal orgasms. Orgasms for women are mainly clitoral. The man who studies this piece of anatomy is on his way to success with his woman, providing paradise for her.

Okay, gentlemen, here's the scoop. Yes, the clitoris is like a little penis, but "little" is the operative word. Get out your sex manuals and find out exactly where it is. Or ask her. She knows. Begin away from it, perhaps pulling the skin on the inside of her thigh. This connects with the delicate tissues around the clitoris and excites her. Then when you have the "car" warmed up, drive slowly toward your goal. The clitoris is the most sensitive and vulnerable part of a woman and handled properly, as the amazing instrument it is, great joy may occur. Learn to pleasure it, and love to love her.

The "G Spot"

In most women there really is the "G Spot." It is highly arousable and located about one inch inside the vagina toward the pubic bone. When you locate it, both of you will know it.

However, a man needs to get the "G Spot" only after he has accomplished some productive foreplay. The skilled man slowly touches her, in no place special at first. Then his hands wander to the outsides of her breast. He is tender, teasing, and has brought her to the place where she wants "more." He caresses her breasts, paying attention to her, doing what he can to arouse her. Some women can be brought to orgasm just by having their breasts fondled. Then he moves on, taking his time around her thighs, moving gently to the labia majora, minor labia, and the clitoris. She may have several orgasms without even knowing what he did, if he has done his female-anatomy homework. Then he moves with his fingers inside her, finding the "G Spot," and bringing her again to orgasm.

What Does a Man Want?

1. For her to know that a man is turned on by what he sees and also by what he cannot exactly see. So a bit of cleavage, a show of leg, tight jeans and a sexy walk — do make a difference.

2. That she provide him with a bit of mystery — flirt with him, tease him, and then refuse. Remember the old line, "Say 'no,' say, 'maybe,' but 'yes' is not said directly by a lady." She goes very slowly and knows where she is going, not making it too easy. Remember he is innately a "hunter." Note: "Hunters do not hunt chickens who just sit and wait." Part of the thrill of the hunt is the evasiveness of the prey.

3. Sexually, should he be coming on in his jet plane rate of speed, she pulls away. He likes to pursue. She arranges the pursuit.

4. That women decide on many of the social and relationship issues. After courtship, he tires of making all those entertainment decisions, and hoping that he pleases her. She knows that women are the relationship masters and acts on it.

5. After the marriage, things change from courtship days when both presented their best. Instead of being the hunter, talking with a purpose, listening intently, he now may revert to his natural need

for time alone in his cave watching television or reading the newspaper.

6. He wants her to not count on him for everything. He also wants her to keep those female friends for long talks so she does not expect him to listen to and empathize with all issues.

7. That she learn from him in bed and teach him gently about her desires. (Couples need to constantly learn about and teach each other, without making the other wrong.) For her to say, "Ohhh, that feels so good when you stroke my thigh, and don't get too close." For her to know that he feels great about himself when he gives her pleasure.

8. He is very sensitive about his penis. He is often awed by it and his inability to know what it will and will not do, and to control it. He wants her to speak about how it pleasures her and never speak about it in a disparaging way, even in heated arguments.

9. That she initiate sometimes when she approaches him, telling him with her whispers and touch that she wants him. This can be especially provocative in places that he cannot have her, like restaurants, airplanes, or the movies.

10. To know that his sexual needs are quicker and more to the point than hers. Once in a while it's sexy to just go fast.

The Magnificent Penis

Men are in awe of this part of themselves and very protective of it. Many men complain that women are ignorant of how the penis works, as many women complain that men are ignorant of the clitoris. Learning about how the other is pleasured equals love and respect.

Most men love to be aroused either by a woman's hands or mouth. They are proud of the erect penis. After all, from this are sired generations of people. The man is built and organized to spread his seed. The erect penis is the symbol of his fertility. In days of old, kings were killed or asked to step down when they became old and past virility. It was feared that if a king could not sire and produce children, the realm would also become infertile and unprosperous.

The more the woman honors, exalts, and knows about the pleasures of the man's penis, the more she intrigues him. The more she becomes the mistress of the mysteries of his most vulnerable and unpredictable penis, the more he adores her. So it is wise for a woman to learn which parts are most sensitive, which parts cause him ecstasy. She needs to read her sexual anatomy books, and then use her hands and/or other parts of her body, or mouth, to please him.

The Head of the Penis

Okay, ladies, your turn. Grab your pens. Like the "G Spot," the head of the penis (the glans) is a great place of arousal. However, like the clitoris, it must not be approached quickly nor roughly. The glans is almost the representation of the way a woman is with the man. This is the most delicate area of his anatomy, and must be approached slowly and gently. First, the woman pleasures whatever parts of him she has discovered are pleasing to him. Then she pleasures the penis, the scrotum, and then finally, when he is ready, she pleases the delicate rim. She drives him to rapture.

Many Eastern books on sexuality exalt and ritualize sexuality, emphasizing a knowledge of sensitive areas of anatomy. Books like these need to be in every couple's library.

CHAPTER 8

Parenting - Men and Women Parent Differently

QUIZ 8: HOME, FAMILY, AND PARENTING

Instructions: Photocopy the quiz and each fill it out without discussion. It is best to work quickly. Answer, don't think. Then compare your results with the information tables in the back of the book.

Do you or are you:

1 = Always
2 = Usually
3 = Sometimes
4 = Seldom
5 = Never

Section A — Parenting:

1. _____ consider mother's/father's teachings to be different from one another?

2. _____ teach boys and girls using different techniques for each?

3. _____ talk little but expect children to learn by watching you?

4. _____ teach children by talking and doing?

5. _____ inclined to be authoritative?

6. _____ naturally nurture children?

7. _____ talk with children about their behavior?

8. _____ believe that "the buck stops here?"

Section B — Home and Family:

9. _____ consider how your home looks is a reflection of yourself?

10. _____ send greeting cards often?

11. _____ plan holiday gatherings?

12. _____ move place of residence with relative ease?

13. _____ view home simply as a place to live?

14. _____ interested in maintaining the mechanical structure of home?

15. _____ like to work with tools around the house?

16. _____ like to plan and purchase home furnishings?

17. _____ like to plan and execute house and yard improvements?

18. _____ notice others' home furnishings?

19. _____ fix broken things in the house and yard?

20. _____ enjoy caring for indoor plants?

21. _____ make appointments for health care for other family members?

22. _____ like to go and buy the new car?

Children

He:
Reprimands the children for not doing something well. Establishes the order "Not good enough, do it again." or "Right now." No negotiations, no reasons, "Just do it."

She:
Interest is primarily in relating, guiding, and protecting the concept of a safe haven called home.

He:
Dad teaches the ways of the hunt, the ways of the work place, the ways of a hierarchy, the rules of the game and how it is played. Dad backs up Mom with a look or a strong voice.

She:
Mother instructs children in manners, mores, chores, family and social values, and ethics. Mom usually urges everyone to go to church or synagogue. She sets standards of faith and values of trust and good citizenship, respect for the church and God, and a cohesiveness with the values of the community.

He:
Roughhouses with the children.

She:
Wants things less noisy, fears he will hurt the children with his form of play.

When questioned about the children he was watching, says, "Oh they were here just a few minutes ago."

Is always on the alert for them, constantly scanning, listening.

Nurturing Styles

Nurtures by solving the problem. He goes to get the facts and lines up the difficulties, focusing his attention on the difficulty *out there.*

Talks. She empathizes with the other's feelings. She soothes, offers food or aspirin, focusing on the inside.

CHAPTER 9

How We Hurt Each Other

QUIZ 9: HURTING EACH OTHER OFTEN ABOUT MONEY OR POWER

Instructions: Photocopy the questions. Work apart from your partner. Do not compare results until the end. Work quickly. This should take no more than two minutes to complete. Compare with each other and then compare with the information in the back of the book.

Do you or are you:

1 = Always
2 = Usually
3 = Sometimes
4 = Seldom
5 = Never

Money and Power

1. _____ like to think of yourself as courageous?

2. _____ view war as necessary?

3. _____ like to be thought of as forceful?

4. _____ comfortable expressing strong views in a confrontational manner?

5. _____ proud of your physical strength?

6. _____ fear being thought of as angry?

7. _____ defer to another's opinion readily?

8. _____ like being viewed as an aggressive person?

9. _____ dislike the thought of war?

10. _____ like to compete in many areas of life?

11. _____ find yourself "giving away" your power to your partner in life?

12. _____ prefer to "do good" than earn a lot of money?

13. _____ care little if you earn less money than your partner?

How We Even the Score: Solutions that Don't Work

Passive Aggression

At times in every relationship there will arise a struggle for power and control. Either partner may handle such conflict in a way therapists label as Passive Aggressive.

The DSM (the Diagnostic and Statistical Manual of Mental Disorders, the manual therapists use to diagnose emotional disorders) defines a Passive Aggressive as "one who is resistant to demands for adequate performance in occupational and social functioning; the resistance is expressed indirectly rather than directly." Passive Aggressive people resent and oppose demands to increase or maintain a given level of functioning.

The manual descibes a person as Passive Aggressive if he or she demonstrates even two of the following behaviors:

- procrastination
- dawdling
- stubbornness
- intentional inefficiency
- forgetfulness

The DSM gives as examples the person who always comes late to appointments, the one who promises to help make arrangements for particular events but never does, and the person who keeps "forgetting" to bring documents to club meetings; all passively resisting demands made by others.

The act of not doing is subtly aggressive and controlling. Being unable or unwilling to show anger or aggression with an immediacy and in an active way, the Passive Aggressive person expresses the aggressiveness in a passive way. Instead of openly arguing an issue through to some conclusion, for example, he or she will terminate the discussion by shutting up and becoming silent. Silence is an extremely effective weapon. It is so powerful it may have the effect of increasing the other's anger to a tirade, or may cause the other to give up and walk away.

A woman comes home from work. She says, "We need milk for the baby. He's really hungry. Will you go and get it?" He says he will. She waits, asks him about the milk. He says, "I'll go in a minute. Stop bugging me."

The man uses the bathroom sink and finds hair and makeup all over the counter top. He and his wife have had constant fights about this. She says she forgot.

This woman and man, often, without consciously realizing what they are doing, harbor anger in a deep and slow simmer. When anger is not recognized and expressed, it builds, abscesses, and may lead to an explosion.

Often, however, it is expressed in Passive Aggressive ways — forgetting, dawdling, stonewalling, and silence. Individuals become Passive Aggressive because they believe that in their families of origin or in later primary relationships other direct forms of communication did not work.

Learning each other's languages will help partners avoid this damaging form of communication.

Abusive Relationships — Verbal, Financial, Emotional, or Spiritual

What is an abusive relationship? Today, physical abuse is clearly understood, but we find that people don't recognize other types of abuse, even when they are subjected to them. Here are some examples:

1. Scott Peck, in his famous book, *The Road Less Traveled*, writes that relationships must exist for the "highest good of the other." When one does not allow for the other's purpose and well-being, there is a kind of abuse.

We have heard women complain that men work too much and give too much attention to that work, leaving little for her or the children. It is important to know what he is doing is the nature of the hunter/warrior. He judges himself by comparison to other hunters/warriors. Is this abusive, or is he just being a good hunter? Is the woman pushing him to do too much at home? What is his job as a partner/father? Define these things together.

The huntress, the executive woman, is also manifesting herself today. Many successful women are losing their marriages when the men find they cannot control them and want them at home. These men must understand that women working outside the home is a natural part of today's economy. Men who demean successful women may feel abused by them because they are not home and taking care of the men. Some men feel threatened and may become abusive.

Both men and women must allow the other what is his or her highest good.

2. Assets and monies of the man and the woman must be worked out in any successful partnership. Either one trying to control the finances, works against the other. We often see women or men with financial assets enmesh with each other. They enter marriage with money, but no prenuptial agreement, or any other agreement as to how their financial lives will work together. This situation creates unrealistic expectations and notions of entitlement.

Money and other assets are an integral part of the workings of the partnership. When one has a greater salary and contributes more of the finances to the partners' lives, the question of how the other's contributions of time and energy compensates, certainly must be made clear.

The romantic notion that "it will all work out" does not work today. Agreements must be worked out between the partners. They must clearly define jobs, responsibilities, expectations, and allocation of time, energy, and money.

3. The use of time must be agreed upon. One or the other will resent what appears to be unequal fun time, such as television, the gym, or friends. Allocation of time must be agreed to, complete with full knowledge of gender differences and needs.

Shaming and Blaming

We have written about this, but we cannot emphasize enough the necessity of not blaming the other for what happens in the partnership. In any partnership, both are responsible. Blame only makes the "blamer" wrong, the "blamee" wrong, and the relationship wrong. Such blame can become a justification for abuse in the abuser's mind. In fact, shaming another in itself is verbal abuse! One person does something inappropriate. Too often, the partner shames the person for the act, instead of trying to understand and work out the problem with non-threatening conversation like, "I see what you did as . . ." or "I feel like . . . when you . . ."

Too often, instead of taking responsibility for changing our behavior or for claiming our own feelings about another's behavior, we shame our partner's very being with our words — all for that one act. Also, we dig out old issues, and add them to the shame we pile on our partner. Nothing is learned. Nothing positive is accomplished. We need to stop it!

Something goes amiss when we don't take responsibility for the wholeness and health of the partnership. We are grownups now. Our children are watching, and will do the same awful acts we do. They learn by our model of adulthood, and by our positive attempts to work on ourselves and on the partnership.

For our childen's sake and for our own, we must retrain ourselves to explore non-abusive, non-blaming responses to our partner's actions. Jeannette tells a wonderful story of a time when she observed her husband's mother choosing a different way. "Mommy Lofas' " gentle and loving reaction to a potentially explosive situation should serve as a model for us all.

Mommy Lofas, the Five-Second Manager

This is a story I often tell men and women who are very much concerned about what is fair and unfair behavior between married couples. It is a story of how one person — in this case, a woman — handled a potentially explosive situation with dignity and strength.

Returning from our honeymoon, my husband and I stopped in Sweden to visit his parents, whom I called Mommy and Daddy Lofas. They were a loving couple and had, at the time, been married over thirty years. He was very handsome, with white hair and a mustache and spoke English with a British accent. She, Marta, was beautiful. She had dark hair and violet eyes that twinkled with wit and wisdom.

Daddy Lofas had brought our suitcases upstairs and placed them in the front hall of the apartment and had gone off to do something. After a few minutes, he came back and raised his voice at Mommy Lofas. I had never heard him do this, and could not understand why he was taking this tone with her.

"Marta, why are those suitcases in the front hall?" he shouted. She looked away from him to me. She smiled and winked at me. It seemed she was about to teach me something. "Oh, oh, Alf," she said in a soft voice, "where do you want me to put the suitcases?" He gumbled and grunted. Then he firmly told her that the suitcases belonged in the bedroom and that they were too heavy for her, and he would take them there himself. She looked at me again and smiled.

The family was blissful and calm again. At the time, had it been my husband treating me that way, I would have told him indignantly that, indeed, he had put the suitcases in the hallway, and I would be damned if I would let him talk to me in that way. Especially since he was wrong. This might have caused a two-hour or a two-day fight.

What Mommy Lofas taught me was how to be a five-second manager. What she did completely in the five-second transaction was what we now call "going over the top of the situation" instead of confronting it directly. She pursued her desired outcome and didn't let the barrier of her husband's momentary impoliteness stop her.

CHAPTER 10

Why?

It is a lie that men and women, except for a few particular features of plumbing, are the same. Men and women are as different as a line and a circle. One cannot be the other. Instead of recognizing this fact and respecting the differences, men and women often blame each other. Other couples have sought to manage difficult relationships through counseling, therapy, and volumes of advice written by hundreds of "experts."

This advice has not worked. The success rate of marriage counselors is about fifty percent — the exact number of couples, according to the U.S. Census, who divorce anyway.

The War Between the Sexes Goes On and On!

The problem is that both men and women are threatened by gender differences. The reality is that these very differences have provided both male and female achievements and genius throughout the ages. Indeed, these differences must be held in high esteem.

Since the eighties, we have new scientific information about gender differences. With this new information, we now have the opportunity to take advantage of the particular ways, views, and talents of men and women. Anything else is a sheer waste of the genius of our species.

Joan's Story: My New Knowing About Gender Revived Our Marriage

My own marriage of many years was in trouble when Jeannette and I began working on this book. I was called an expert in communication skills, and yet I could not communicate with my own husband. He would stonewall, saying that I surrounded him in too many words. I said he shut me out. Successful in our professions, we felt like failures in our relationship.

Information began unfolding. Men are unilateral thinkers: left-brained, problem solving, cognitive, brief, and to the point. Men think something through and say it once. Women switch back and forth quickly, emotions readily accessible, talking through ideas, switching from this topic to that. Women are not reluctant to be emotional because they get in and out of their emotions easily. For men this is difficult. Men interrupt to express interest. They show interest by disagreeing.

Testosterone! It was with relief that we discovered that neither way is right or wrong. We are supposed to think and communicate and do things differently because we are different in every cell and chemical in our bodies! I actually began admiring Dave's generous supply of testosterone. He began realizing that, in spite of my aggressive approach to the business world, I really was tremendously feminine in my abilities to talk, and talk, and talk. Our expectations of each other became more realistic, many of our arguments changed to chuckles.

Celebrate our differences? Now that we understand them, "Yes!"

Confusion Caused by the Norm of "Male Values" Only

Our current world has become more masculine, less feminine. Talk such as "Plundering the forests, hostile take-overs, robbing the earth, and building missiles instead of schools . . ." are indeed gender arguments.

We agree that the male norms of the hunter-warrior are to be respected, and that today's economics mandate that many women must work whether they want to or not.

However, results of this lack of gender balance can be disastrous.

The Feminist Movement and A Loss of the Feminine Values

We believe a major fault of the Feminist Movement was that, without meaning to, it put down feminine characteristics and attributes. In psychology, we know those who are abused either identify with the aggressor or with the victim.

The Women's Movement took its values from the male. The male, however, was often labeled as the aggressor. The movement encouraged women to become more like men. It rallied women to free themselves from male oppression in order to achieve equality, yet it embraced the very values that led to that oppression rather than demanding a balance be struck with feminine values. Male values are not wrong; they just need to be kept in check by an equal reverence for female values in society. Like everything in nature, success between genders requires balance.

In the past few decades, millions of women left home and went to work.

What was traditionally the woman's vital domain — the home, the children, social life, values, and the family — to this day remains largely unattended. Most men still do not pick up the tasks and values of the home.

On the Other Hand: The Men's Movement, A Praising of the Male Way of Being

The Men's Movement began in the late eighties and reached its apex in the early nineties. Unlike women, men praised the characteristics of their own sex, such as being good providers, protectors, and hunters. To affirm their maleness, they met in the woods for weekends. They pounded drums, acted fierce, told stories, and dealt with the sorrow of absent fathers. They focused their attention on getting to know what being "a man" really was. Women were neither exalted nor put down.

The focus was on the essence of maleness. The Men's Movement took a look at men. The Woman's Movement also looked at men, and turned away from women's own ways of being.

Too Often, Therapy Has Not Helped!

Originally the field of therapy was grounded in thousands of hours of case studies based on work with women. The vast majority of patients of the fathers of psychiatry, psychology, social work — Freud, Adler, and Jung — were women. To communicate with women and their world view, some of these men learned to speak like women. They learned a woman's way of thinking and speaking, what we call "Femalese."

Femalese Says, "How Do You Feel About That?"

Still today, highly skilled professionals speak this female-based language and order their way of thinking around the female mode of being, emoting, and valuing. The focus is on the internal. The classic question is, "How do you feel?" In general, much of today's therapy deals with feelings and relationships and not with tasks.

Women often enjoy talking about their feelings. Feelings are not at all threatening to them, and they most often do not understand why feelings can be threatening to males.

Malese Says, "How Do We Get It Done?"

This female world view is markedly different from the more male directed approach of expressing concepts, or "Malese." In Malese one would ask,

"What is the task?" "How do we do it?" "Who and what do we need to get it done?" The journalistic five W's — who, what, why, when, and where are good examples of Malese, in which the focus is most often external.

CHAPTER 11

Solutions, Tools

Any fruitful discussion between men and women requires that both genders have some understanding of how the opposite gender communicates. Here are some suggestions for productive communication based on the differences we have been discussing:

To Women: How to Understand Men's Ways of Communicating

1. KIS, or "Keep it simple."

2. Stay on one topic at a time. It drives men crazy when women switch from one idea to another. Men are left-brained and tend to prefer linear talk, sequential ideas.

3. Do not be offended if a man does not consistently look at you while you talk. Remember, men often face outward and talk in a parallel position.

4. Expect interruptions. Interrupting is his way of showing interest. Attentive listening, nodding the head, making listening noises is a female way of showing interest.

5. Expect distracting behaviors. A man can walk around the room and keep talking. This is not meant as an insult to you.

6. Men like to be "right." Coming on strongly may threaten a man and cause him to react defensively, aggressively, or withdraw.

7. The best way to say something significant, even potentially threatening, is directly and slowly. You should think it out before speaking, so you can say it just once.

8. When you smile and act agreeably in the work place, a man may take this as flirtatious behavior. His response may have sexual overtones. You might gently clarify how much you value him as a colleague and friend at work.

9. Do not direct a man. Refrain from saying "Do this. Do that." This can be difficult for women in the work place with male subordinates.

10. Keep your sense of humor.

To Men: How to Understand Women's Ways of Communicating

1. Remember, the woman speaks twice as many words as you do.

2. When you come home you probably do not want to relate through words. Perhaps you are out of words; you gave at the office. She, on the other hand, wants to relate — she's got all these words left to speak. Set a time with her every night when you can communicate for at least 15 minutes, alone.

3. Distracting behaviors such as looking through magazines or fidgeting with something may very well cause a woman to be upset with you. She yearns for direct, eye-to-eye, soul-to-soul communication.

4. Interrupting to show interest is okay with men. Women, however, may find it rude and even domineering.

5. Women have easy access to both sides of the brain — the left (linear) and the right (intuitive and feeling). Women may "drive men crazy" with their right and left brain switching. If you find yourself unable to track her conversation, work on not falling

prey to your natural tendency to withdraw. Instead, be pro-active. Ask her to stick to one topic at a time.

6. Women talking to women may seem outrageous, breaking all of all the rules (men's linear rules — A, B, C). "Do not go to L and don't forget D." The female brain allows her to wander, often making no sense to a male. You may not be able to learn the female way of speaking, but do respect the versatility of the female mind.

7. Guiding the relationship, as women often do, is easily perceived by you as being bossed. State your need to not be guided or directed. Tell her that for eons, it was the lower ranking male who was told what to do by the higher-ranking male. Tell her that it is hard for you to be told "how to…," "where to…," "or what to…"

8. If you feel that she is nagging you, do a little self-checking: "Do I feel bossed around by her? Does it seem she is saying the same thing over and over again, so all I want to do is pull away?" Say so. Tell her how you wish she would talk with you. We don't have to use the old, domineering routine. We do have to learn to communicate.

9. When she says something that results in your feeling angry or withdrawn, say back to her what you heard her say, as best you can. Try to use a neutral tone and say, "Let's try to clarify what we're saying to each other, rather than fight."

10. Keep your sense of humor.

How to Have Successful Discussions:

The reason partners converse is to get closer to each other, to understand one another better, and to get things accomplished. If they didn't care, they wouldn't engage in discussions, especially not ones about difficulties and misunderstandings. Therefore, think about looking at a discussion as an act of love. The following is a list of suggestions, things to keep in mind in order to focus on the real purpose of a discussion — to grow closer.

Dos

1. **Know each gender's different ways of communicating.** Partnership is about learning these and taking best advantage of them.

2. **If this is the time and place, discuss.** Don't duck. Don't attack. Remember this is a discussion, not a battle. Recognize that two intelligent people do have differences. Different points of view need to be talked about, not buried. Strive for solutions and/or an agreement to disagree.

3. **Remember that the goal is relationship, not winning.** Discussions are not done to win. Winning is the "booby prize" in successful partnerships. Retire your "score boards."

4. **Refrain from litigating your issues with evidence.** This most often causes the other to match with contrary evidence and can lead to vicious debates and arguments. Partnerships are not court rooms. Right and wrong is of little value in a good partnership. Go for an outcome which results in the highest good for the couple.

5. **Attempt to help yourself and the other person to stay focused on the one issue.** Often artistic and creative men or women have a thinking style which wanders. Remind yourselves to stick with the issue. Speak from your heart. Don't criticize.

6. **Stick to the present.** Refrain from bringing in examples from the past. Anything older than 72 hours is the past.

7. **Calling a "time out."** Should either feel too irritated or overwhelmed, make an agreement to call a time out. Agree to continue the discussion at another time.

8. **Don't be afraid to give in.** Being the peacemaker or conceder for the sake of the relationship is a sign of strength. Scott Peck in *The Road Less Traveled* says that each must assist the other in the highest possible way. Go for the "highest" in your relationship.

9. **When you finish one issue take a break,** hug each other, say "Thank you."

10. **Celebrate** — following a resolution, buy each other a gift, send a note, or go out on the town. This is called positive reinforcement. It encourages each partner to work with the other in solving problems.

11. Use the AB Reality tool (See chapter 12.) to make discussions work. Remember discussions are about honoring each other. Use "I . . ." messages. Arguments dishonor both people and the relationship. Arguments use "you . . ." messages, which are: accusing, blaming, loud and pushy, and do not honor the purpose of the relationship — closeness, intimacy, and caring.

Don'ts

1. **Don't start with "I want to talk to you."** This phrase automatically engenders a defensive reaction which often stems from childhood when this phrase meant you had done something wrong.

2. **Do not call names** or assassinate each other's character.

3. **Don't "triangulate."** That is, don't bring in any other person or issue: experts, quotes from scripture, in-laws, or the like. Women tend to triangulate because many issues come up for them. Men tend to triangulate to prove their point.

4. **Don't generalize.** Be specific. Give examples. Talk about how it looks, sounds, and feels to you.

5. **Don't "hit below the belt."** Because belt-lines (things too hurtful to talk about) are so different for males and females, each person will have to recognize his or her own, and tell the other clearly what they are. To "hit below the belt" can be verbally abusive and invite rage or withdrawal.

6. **Do not threaten to end the relationship.** This is hitting below the belt, and in a relationship is a "cheap shot."

7. **Don't go to bed angry.** Develop some bedtime ritual, such as praying or reading aloud to each other, so that you don't.

8. **Don't use "always," "never," "should," and "ought."** It's a rule for good relationships.

9. **Don't raise your voice.** Often when we do, all the other hears is the process — the raised voice, rather than the content of what we want to get across.

10. **Do not fight within earshot of the children,** unless you are only "discussing." Discussions are OK for kids to hear — fighting is not. Fighting scares the children in this age of divorce.

Steps in Healing Relationships

1. Know the classic issues over which you fight. Is it money? Time? Attention? The children? Television? Feeling ignored?

2. Know how you fight. What bugs you about her/his fighting systems? Work to get discussions on a "level playing field" and solve or get rid of any ways of fighting which one or the other feels is unfair.

3. Know where you usually fight. Have a specific place to fight, in the house, on the street in a "Fighting/Discussing Only" restaurant or coffee shop. Keep the bedroom as an intimate place; do not fight there.

4. Know when and why you usually fight. When: After a hard day of work? When the kids are in bed? When you're tired? Why: Did the other not meet your expectations? Was a promise broken? Are you feeling bad about yourself or the other?

5. Know what the usual outcomes are. Is there a resolution? Do you stop talking to each other? Does the fight flare up for days and then finally die down, solved or unsolved? Then fix new rules for fighting. A successful fight results in problem solving.

6. In our counseling work, we say each must assume 100 percent of the responsibility for a partnership to work. A favorite axiom is: "There are no mistakes in communication, only outcomes." The result of your communication is what she/he heard, saw, or felt. The object, then, is for each to "own" his or her 100 percent, and not blame the other.

7. What education and resources are needed? Resources are necessary to allow discovery of, and re-education regarding what hasn't been working. Is a therapist needed?

8. Celebrate good results. When you do find a positive win/win result, you must validate each other's efforts and celebrate with each other.

9. Know that there cannot be a void in any nature, least of all in a human being. When anything old moves out, there has to be something to fill the resulting space. When we remove old and unworkable beliefs, or understandings, or behaviors, we have to find and use new and improved ones.

10. Use the exercises, drills, and tools described in Chapter 12.

Getting Our Emotional Needs Met

Every man and woman has three basic emotional needs. First is *Validation*, the need to be "noticed" and loved. Second is *Community*, the need to have support systems; people who care about us. Third is *Excitement*, the inclusion of variety and interest in our lives. These are needs, not wants. Essentially all of our behavior is an attempt to get these needs met.

When our emotional needs do not feel met, discouragement sets in. This is acted out below our conscious awareness, subconsciously. We play out our unhappiness in what appear to be "misbehaviors."

The first level of discouraging misbehaviors is doing annoying things.

The second level is an increase or escalation of behaviors such as picking fights and abusive language. For many, getting revenge is a part of this stage.

Third and finally, we give up — leaving the relationship, attempting to anesthetize feelings, or even committing suicide.

Solutions:

Understanding this, the task we have as adults is to take responsibility for the fulfillment of our own needs. Too often we expect these needs will be met by our partner. But the truth is that the responsibility is our own. No one else can fill our needs!

- Self-esteem and self-care are up to us.
- The development of other support systems is up to us. This includes developing same-sex friends to supplement the friendship of our mate. We set ourselves up for disappointment when we expect our mate to fill every need.
- Planning interesting events into every week is up to us. The nature of excitement, or recreation, is to do things that are different from our normal activities. If our job is sedentary, taking a bike ride or going on a power walk helps provide excitement. We can ask, rather than expect, our mate to share some of these events.

In addition, too often we expect the other to "know" our wants, and then we're angry or discouraged if he or she does not. We have to ask if we want help in getting our needs met. This means to clearly put requests into words — no game playing, no relying on unspoken clues.

Guidelines for Male and Female Parenting/Disciplining Together

1. Male and female heads of the household, decide together what the guidelines for the children will be. Remember men and women parent differently. Reconcile those differences.

2. Have family meetings. Listen to your children. Make it clear that you do "hear" them. Often it is Mother, with her natural listening and nurturing skills, who listens and interprets children's ideas to Dad. In a remarried family, the female or male role is more difficult, due to the "step" situation, but with mutual support between the parents, this difficulty can be defused.

3. As Mom and Dad constantly evaluate and re-decide what the rules will be, remember each child gets only one vote. Each parent gets 17 votes.

4. Dad is most often the final strong voice.

5. "Don't sweat the small stuff." Mom and Dad, decide together what the small stuff is in your home. We believe things like how tightly the bed is made is an example of "small stuff." Save your "big guns" for big infractions of rules.

6. Clearly state the guidelines to the children. As rules change, tell the children. Post them so children cannot "forget."

7. Should children break the guidelines, have clearly stated consequences ready. For the best results, "the punishment should suit the crime." For example, if the child dawdles and causes the family to be 10 minutes late to an outing, delaying the child's play for 20 minutes to do a household task is a significant lesson.

8. Consequences work. Quietly enforce them.

9. Have positive as well as negative consequences. Reward good jobs and good behavior. At family meetings you and the kids decide what are the positive and negative consequences.

10. When you do have to talk to the child about his/her behavior, say things in a calm, "pass the bread and butter," tone of voice. "Yelling" weakens your point and your power.

11. Children hate hypocrisy. The word discipline comes from the word disciple, meaning to follow after. Children learn from observing their parents and other adults. From Mom they learn manners, mores, family, social values, and ethics. From Dad they learn the ways of the work place, the hierarchy, problem solving, and toughness to the completion of a task.

12. Expect good behavior. This positive atmosphere encourages and results in more frequent appropriate behavior.

13. Praise children for doing anything well. Praise must be specific, low-key, and honest.

14. Refrain from belittling or embarrassing a child. The number one fear in children is the fear of being embarrassed. Put-downs often result in passive-aggressive misbehavior. The subconscious mind causes "I'll show you" behavior.

15. State what the child needs to do, rather than what she or he needs not to do.

16. Guard your sense of humor. Mom and Dad, laugh together. Laugh with, not at, the children.

CHAPTER 12

Exercises, and Drills for Positive Partnering

A, B Reality: The Honoring of Differences and The Beginning of Creating Couple Strength

Lofas relates how she devised the AB Reality Method.

I learned High School History in three German speaking countries. The history was very different in each country. At first, I naively made notes to my teachers that other countries had different versions of the same story. They ignored me. Then I wrote a paper descibing these differences. I got a reprimand, "This was not the assignment!" and a low grade. So I stopped this comparison business. I decided that history was just a point of view and not just the facts, and that it varied country to country, teacher to teacher.

Actually, this rude awakening was not such a bad thing. My divorced parents were still angry at each other. Each constantly told me a different story about the other. My school experiences helped me to deal with the conflicts between my parents. I began to view them just as having experienced history from different points of view. I was relieved of the awful curse, when children often are asked to take sides, of believing one parent over the other.

Instructions: Explaining A, B Reality to my clients, I draw two boxes — one with a big A and the other with a big B. I explain that each of us is programmed differently: A likes pink flowers, B likes red flowers. A does not like to sunbathe, B loves the sun. B argues, "A, you look great with a tan. Come with me to the beach, and let's enjoy the sun together." "No,"says A. "You, B, are a dope to lie in the sun."

Each tries to pull the other into their A or B Reality. Each argues his/her point of view. Arguments sometimes go on for days, even years.

It works to respect the other's point of view. We must create a C reality in a partnership. To do this, we take some from A's reality and some from B's reality. Agreements to disagree are agreements to go into a C column until all is worked out.

Do this by never using the word "You." Language like, "You don't know what you are talking about! This is the reality!" is not allowed. Remember, we are learning to understand and speak different languages— Malese and Femalese. As in a foreign country, showing courtesy in any communication exchange is imperative!

Use the words, " I feel . . . I see . . . I hear . . ." We own and honor the reality as our own. We recognize that the other is not wrong, but simply different.

The Lake Placid Exercise

How We See, Hear, Feel, and Sort our Realities by People, Places, and Things

A story Jeannette tells once again exemplifies differences we have been addressing. Now we look further into how our partners see, hear, and feel the world, and how they sort their realities in terms of people, places, and things.

My husband is the usual guinea pig for the training exercises I learn at professional seminars. Once, after skiing the whole day at Lake Placid, I asked him if he would endure an experiment that would take place during the journey from the door of the hotel to a restaurant where we were dining that night. "Yes," he sighed. With a little trepidation, like the girl with the tea party story related in chapter nine, I filled him in on what was to take place.

"We will see, hear, feel, and sort regarding people, places, and things — everything that takes place during this brief period, without talking or sharing our realities. We'll do that only when we sit down."

"Blessings," he cried, happy that this was to be such an uncomplicated exercise. We followed through with the plan and once seated in the restaurant, he said, "You start." I did.

My Reality:

We went out of the hotel door. It was freezing cold. Ice was on the steps down to the car. He held my arm to help me into the car. "How nice," I thought. "I was falling all over the mountain during the day, and he did not offer to pick me up. Well, we are both tough skiers." I was dressed for dinner. I remember nothing of the drive except the night was black. We pulled into the parking lot, and I could hear the gravel under the car wheels. We walked up the steps to the restaurant. A blond buxom lady led us to our table. I smelled the room, thinking the food would be only mediocre, and looked around at the people — pretty mediocre also.

His Reality:

Bob's turn was next. Interestingly enough, his memory didn't include helping me into the car or the drive to the restaurant. But, after getting to the restaurant through the pitch black of the night (my reality), he did notice how many other BMWs were in the parking lot and that the license plates were from different states. How many from Canada? Massachusetts? New York? Vermont? New Jersey? He did not notice the blond lady who took us to our table.

How different we are. I would never have looked at the men — they spend so much time thinking about how they measure up to other men. Who else had a BMW? How far did others have to drive to get there? While I had heard the parking lot, he saw what was in it. What was I always thinking about? Feelings and people.

Instructions: Drive, walk or go to an occasion and designate 15-20 minutes to not talk, but to just be in the same place together. Then sit down and compare. Have Fun!

Walk a Mile in the Other's Shoes — High Heels or Cordovans

This exercise involves actually becoming your partner's shadow in movement and in spirit. The two of you go for a walk. The walk must be in an area where there are people, stores, or things with which to interact. When your partner stares at something, you stare at the same thing. No matter how long he or she looks at something or interacts with someone, stand by and observe. Attempt to feel what is going on with your partner. What is important to him/her? Why does he/she like to do this? What makes it nice? What is difficult for you? What insights do you have about you and your partner?

This is really getting to know each other by observing, so, NO laughter, unless she/he does, and NO put downs. The follower's job is to be silent and to "be with . . ." The walker's job is to BE him/herself and to do as he/she would normally do. As the follower, in the corner of your mind, as you're observing and giving most of your attention to the other, think about what you like and would want to do or say under the same circumstances.

Walk the way your partner walks. Look at what your partner looks at, feel what he/she touches. Imagine how your partner talks to a salesperson in a store. Stay close, saying nothing. Be a shadow. Your job is to learn, know, imitate, BE your partner. You see, hear, feel as she/he does.

Don't forget to have fun! This is a way your partner and you can find out astonishing similarities and dissimilarities in the way each of you views the world. We may not exactly understand our differences, but we can respect them.

Instructions: This exercise takes about 20 minutes each time. It can be done when you both go for a walk, to the mall, to the seashore, or other places you plan together. Each partner takes a turn. Compare your insights after each is finished. Enjoy.

Fite Fair

This technique is used by stepfamily professionals, but it can also be done by couples at home. It is used when a couple continues to fight about one subject that they seem unable to resolve. Then what is called for is what we refer to as a "fite fair."

Instructions: The fite fair must be held in a totally safe space after the children have gone to bed. It should be done in the basement, in the attic — someplace where the couple will not be disturbed. They go into the space, taking two equally sized chairs, pulling these up close to each other, sitting knee to knee. Both place their hands on their thighs, where the hands will remain so they aren't used in gesturing. Each looks the other partner in the eyes and tries to breathe in sync. This is so that the messages come from soul-to-soul, heart-to-heart, with no movements or gestures which may allow one person to distract or dominate the other.

The person who called the fite fair begins talking. She or he can scream, yell, cry. The other must simply look in the eye, breathe in sync, be with the partner — and not move from the fite fair position. The person who begins can talk as long as he or she wishes, and then when finished says, "I am finished." The other then begins. This partner talks as long as he/she wants to, and when finished, says, "I am finished." The other partner talks once again until finished.

Back and forth this goes, perhaps for thirty minutes. The time between "I am finished," should get shorter so problems can be dealt with, one by one. The couple must endeavor not to string together so many issues that either partner becomes confused or overwhelmed. About thirty minutes into the fite fair, the couple must go for a solution.

They continue to go back and forth until a solution is reached, and THEY MAY NOT GET UP UNTIL THEY AGREE UPON A SOLUTION, EVEN IF THE FITE FAIR TAKES TWO HOURS. In our work with couples, this technique usually takes between an hour and an hour and a half.

The Reason Why This Works Well When Done Effectively

The fite fair technique is best done with a counselor. However, if that is not possible, it can still work to allow venting to be done safely, providing the situation has not grown to unmanageable proportions. Attention has to be given to both partners emotions regarding the subject about which each has previously "made" the other wrong. Through the fite fair, we explain to each other how we feel, how we see it in terms of the A, B Reality Technique, and what we want from the other person. It is an effective form of communication when the couple has reached an impasse.

At the end of a fite fair it is important for the couple to embrace and celebrate the solution.

Calibrating Your Partner:

Does She/He See, Hear, or Feel The World? Neurolinguistic Programming

It is important to learn how your partner, and indeed everyone in your life, is "programmed." Although each of us uses all three of our modalities — seeing, hearing, and feeling — we use one much more frequently than the other two. Is your partner primarily Visual, Auditory, or Feeling/ Kinesthetic (VAK)?

We can determine this simply by watching the other's eyes and listening to his/her verbs. Although not an exact science, and varying between left-and right-handed people, VAK is fast becoming a valuable communication tool in personal life as well as business.

Instructions: Begin calibrating by asking your partner a non-threatening question like, "How was your day?" Visual people's eyes will move up when they are thinking of an old visual event. If they are lying or constructing a visual picture, their eyes will move up left and then up right. If you watch any of the tapes of Nixon talking about Watergate, you will see his eyes move up and left (seeing an old picture) and then up right (constructing his new answer and/or a lie about what he saw). Visual people, when asked to visualize the house they grew up in, look up and left. If we ask them to mentally construct their dream house — we will notice their eyes move to the left and then to the right. (The directions are reversed for left-handed people.) So you see, construction is not always lying. It may just be creating.

When you ask Auditory people how their day was, they may tell you about conversations, or annoyances such as having to endure a loud restaurant at lunch. Their eyes move horizontally — to the left as they talk about old auditory events or tell stories, and to the right as they create new auditory events.

In determining Feeling people — look for eyes which move downward. Often, if they are feeling negative, you'll also see body posture changes (head down, shoulders slumped) when they describe their day. They may relay an encounter with a co-worker, friend, or cab driver — explaining events and ideas in terms of their feelings.

Calibrating your partner, friends, and family will help you understand them better. You can learn to match, i.e., to speak in the same VAK that they do. When you do this, they will receive your message far more readily. For example, if you are communicating with a child who is generally visual, you might say "Johnny, I see that your room is not as orderly as you usually keep it; let's get the picture right and put things where they belong." This gets a lot better results from the visual child than saying, "Johnny didn't you hear me when I said clean up your room?", or "Johnny, I feel really bad that your room is a mess."

There are many courses, books, and seminars on the use of Neuro Linguistic Programming which one might find greatly rewarding for further study.

"Humor Me"

Arguments often occur, frustrations build, and relationships are damaged, because one person tries to convince the other not only to "do it this way," but to understand the rationale as to why this way is "right." The argument goes on because the other cannot understand, and so they will not change either their attitude or actions until they do understand. The result is a continued argument and hurt feelings.

Instructions Are Demonstrated in Joan's story:

Renée and Josh were in their early thirties and had been married five years, quickly having four children. She was an architect, but chose to stay home with the children during their early years. Josh was a financial advisor, working long hours, and providing well for his young family. The two agreed to live on Josh's income.

Renée wanted Josh to demonstrate affection to her when he got home from a day's work. She said this many times, and in our first counseling session stressed her need for this. He said he had worked hard, had been nice to people all day, had the children to greet, and just wanted to "kick back" and watch the news on TV. He had talked enough for the day.

I explained that men and women approach things differently. To a woman, the expression of love means hugs and kisses and talking. To a man, love means providing material things, which Josh was doing very well. Gender stuff!

Because of these gender differences, it's often hard to get the other's viewpoint. I suggested instead, that Renée and Josh try the "Humor me" technique.

"Josh, " I said, role-playing Renée, "I'm frustrated. I appreciate that you provide a good living for us. And, when you get home, I really need you to focus on me for a few minutes, and I need a hug. Then drop into your chair in front of the TV. Just humor me."

Playing Josh, I said to Renée, "Honey, I'm really tired when I get home. Come over and give me a hug, then give me a few minutes to chill out in front of the TV, and then we will talk. Just humor me."

This couple came for counseling just a few times. They had all the basics for a great relationship — love, respect, mutual goals, and similar ideals. The lesson was that neither had to make the other understand the detail of everything in order to ask for and receive something which was very important to them.

Allowing Time for Space in Our Togetherness

Kahlil Gibran, author of *The Prophet*, tells us, "let there be space in our togetherness." The reasons for this are at least twofold:

All Our Eggs In One Basket

First, it is a mistake for either half of a couple to expect everything from the other. We tell clients how shaky it is to put all their eggs in one basket. In addition to the emotional investment in their mate, they also need to have same-sex and other-sex friends. Should any of us expect that one person can be everything to us, we set ourselves up for disappointments.

Cave Time

Second, a man's cycles absolutely require time-outs for him. Eons ago, a man retired to the cave or to a cliff to be alone where he could think things through. Men continue to need this time out. Often when things get heated, a man will become quiet and withdraw from his mate. When he does this, the woman thinks she has done something wrong. She wants to get him to talk about it when the man may need space right then. Her insistence does not work.

Women need to know that the man cannot do without his "cave" times. She needs to let him go off and be alone during these times. Perhaps this is a good time to call a woman friend to talk about what is going on. He needs to tell her when his cave times are, and that these are "about him" rather than wrongdoing on her part. He must put into words that he will be back and that they can talk later. That later, the time for talking, must really happen.

When Women Get Emotional

The opposite is true of a woman. When she gets upset, she wants to vent, to talk, now. If he cannot listen now, at least he needs to set a time to talk. Men often take women's upsets to be their "fault." The woman must tell him it is not his fault.

Together Time

Men, when you do listen, give her your full attention. And tell her when you do not understand her. Ask her to clarify and be more specific so you can understand what she wants.

Instructions: Recognize that timing is different for a man and a woman. Respect these differences. Talk about them together, requesting just what you need from your partner.

Sending and Receiving in Malese and Femalese

One couple we know conducts discussions by telephone. When something important comes up, she actually leaves the home and calls him from the car phone or from a pay phone. They've found what we've known — every statement made by one member of a couple needs a verbal response from the other. Ma Bell forces us to do that. Non-verbal responses, or no-response responses cause inaccurate receipt of messages, and often leave the speaker feeling unheard and unimportant.

Because we tend to hear things in the context of our own experience, and from the perspective of our own gender, it is helpful to say back what we heard the other person say. Time and again people act on what they think the other said. Time and again, when we re-examine a conversation in the counseling office, the intent was entirely different from the way it was received.

"You said I was stupid to make that charge-card purchase!"

"Honey, I said we can't go on making charges, with the interest mounting up like it is."

Instructions: When your mate says something in an important conversation, say it back. "What I heard you say was . . . " If it was not accurate, simply ask your mate to say it again. A good phrase to use is just that, "Say again." Another phrase to use, if the message is difficult to understand is, "Help me understand. Say it another way."

As you practice this, you'll find that both of you will "get" the other's messages more and more accurately. You will also begin listening with more intent to hear just what the person said.

"Turn the Page"

When Jeannette was younger and still believed in androgyny, she was offended when she felt her husband gave advice instead of listening to her. She would complain to her mother in tears, saying that her husband didn't care. She did not know his responses were "about him" and about the way he was formed, and not "about her" at all.

Again and again, Jeannette's mother would say, "Don't bother a man with that. Talk to a woman." Mother would repeat, "Turn the page...Just turn the page."

Joan tells clients that it is important to mature out of "the adolescent need to tell all." When we are "young," at whatever age that is for us, too many of us think we can say everything that comes to mind. Uncensored, we outburst all our thoughts to our mate. The result is often hurt feelings, or anger as the other retaliates.

Instructions: Some of the time, old sayings are true. "Count to ten before you speak." "Turn it over." "Hold your tongue." We add that, while it is important to talk and to share your reality and your life with your partner, it is also necessary to not say some things that come to mind.

When you do need to get something off your chest, call a good same-sex friend. Join a group. Write in a journal. Talk aloud to yourself. Talk aloud to God. Then forget it. "Turn the page."

Calling a Ten

Calling a "ten" is a linear, male solution to medium sized and small differences. Let's say I want to eat Italian and he wants Chinese. We ask each other to give a number. I say that Italian is about a four for me, and he says Chinese is about a seven. So we eat Chinese.

When Jeannette was doing the talk show circuit after the publication of her first book, she was really getting lonely going from city to city. One Friday she had a show in Cleveland and, looking at her husband's calendar, she knew he was free. She said, "I am calling a ten. I cannot spend one more night without you. Go with me to Cleveland." He looked at her and said, "Okay," and winked. "This is your game, darling, and you now owe me a ten." He continued, "Do you remember those clients of mine from Texas — the ones you find so boring? They're coming to town next week for meetings and dinner with their wives. I would like you to book out from your clients, and come to dinner with us that night." He knew she could have found a way not to go to dinner with those people, but it was obviously important to him that she did.

Jeannette got her ten. Her husband got his ten.

Instructions: For some quick solutions call your number, from one to ten. This male, linear number system works in a simple and effective way. When you do call a ten, you must be prepared that your partner has a "chit" on you, with the right to also call a ten for something he or she wants badly.

Calling a "Time Out"

Instructions: Often when we discuss things with each other, one or the other wants to persist and pursue. The other may feel overwhelmed and start to fight or withdraw. Before either begins to yell or argue, it is helpful to call a "time-out." This can be done with pre-arranged hand signals, perhaps the ones used by referees in football games, or with pre-arranged words — which stop the action.

When a time-out is called, it is a must to decide on another specific time when the discussion will be resumed. Make that date, and allow each other the time out.

Date Night

After the first romantic stage of a relationship, couples get bogged down in the mundane. The first bloom diminishes, and many feel they have lost some of the intense love they shared.

Often, since the couple "fell in love" at one time, the qualities which led to the initial attraction are still there. With tenacity, time, and improved communication that love can be rekindled.

Instructions: The couple plans and keeps an evening out together every week. Understanding that this may be financially and logistically hard, this is still prioritized into each week. The evening must be no shorter than three hours, and must be spent on neutral ground. It cannot be at home. A public place like a restaurant modifies the intensity of tempers which might flare at home, and reduces distractions there. The time must be focused on the couple, so this isn't the time for a movie or another couple.

Janet and Fred

One married couple we worked with had grown very far apart, to the extent that they had stopped talking together at all, except briefly about necessities. Janet's and Fred's arguments had given way to a far more serious problem in communication, and that was a stony silence. This couple did not want to spend any more money on fixing their relationship, which they believed had little chance anyway. We told them to take walks, an activity which cost no money at all. We advised them to walk no fewer than three times a week, and for no less than forty-five minutes each time.

They returned to counseling the first two weeks to report that the exercise was stupid, and they were simply walking in angry silence. We told them to put that anger into words as they walked. They began doing that, both saying how they felt. The feelings underneath the anger, more tender ones, began to be expressed. After several more weeks, they spent counseling time talking about those softer feelings and about mutual goals still ahead for them.

And they all lived happily ever after.

APPENDIX

Quiz Answers and Explanations

Quiz 1

Section A — Getting Started

This quiz simply reflects your current gender knowledge, according to our premise. Our premise is that gender differences are "mostly" physiological and hormonal and only to "some degree," affected by environment and nurturing.

Therefore, the possible answers would be:

1. 5
2. 5
3. 5
4. 5
5. 5
6. 1
7. 1
8. 1
9. 2
10. Individual response

Section B — Getting Started, Rate Yourself in Problems with the Opposite Sex

For the majority, in questions 1 — 12, Females will rate as problems they have with males:

Affection
Communication
Money

For the majority, in questions 1 — 12, males will rate as problems they have with females:

Communication
Criticism
Making Decisions

For the majority, in questions 1 — 12, both sexes will rate as problems:

Communication
Control
Sex
Stepchildren
Criticism
Not knowing why the others do what they do

Questions 13 — 34 are for your own insights. Note that Communication appears in each problem set.

Quiz 2 — Differences and Development

We realize no man or woman is at either end of the gender spectrum. None of us is "all male" or "all female."

For the sake of this test, however, we have noted most common "male" responses and "female" responses. They are as follows:

	Female	Male
1.	4, 5	1, 2
2.	4, 5	1, 2
3.	1, 2	4, 5
4.	4, 5	1, 2
5.	1, 2	4, 5
6.	4, 5	1, 2
7.	1, 2	4, 5
8.	4, 5	1, 2
9.	1, 2	4, 5

Quiz 3 — True-False Answers to Knowing the Differences

1. True. Men have fewer, very concentrated sweat glands. Women seem to get "dewy" because their glands are spread all over.
2. False. There's a reason that Mommies hear the baby crying while Daddies sleep right through it. Women are more sensitive to sound. But men are more sensitive to light.
3. True. But women have more mathematical disabilities by the time they get to high school.
4. True. 8% men versus 0.5% women are color blind. Let her pick out the drapes.
5. True. That's one reason that more women than men survived concentration camps.

Quiz 4 — Work and Play

Common "male" and "female" responses are as follows:

	Male	Female
1.	1, 2	4, 5
2.	4, 5	1, 2
3.	1, 2	4, 5
4.	1, 2	4, 5
5.	4, 5	1, 2
6.	1, 2	4, 5
7.	4, 5	1, 2
8.	4, 5	1, 2
9.	1, 2	4, 5
10.	4, 5	1, 2

Quiz 5 — How You Communicate

Section A — About You

	Male	Female
1.	4, 5	1, 2
2.	4, 5	1, 2
3.	1, 2	4, 5
4.	4, 5	1, 2
5.	1, 2	4, 5
6.	1, 2	4, 5
7.	4, 5	1, 2
8.	1, 2	4, 5
9.	4, 5	1, 2
10.	1, 2	4, 5
11.	4, 5	1, 2
12.	4, 5	1, 2
13.	1, 2	4, 5
14.	1, 2	4, 5

Section 2 — Couple Relationship

15.	4, 5	1, 2
16.	4, 5	1, 2
17.	1, 2	4, 5
18.	1, 2	4, 5

Quiz 6 — Love

	Male	Female
1.	4, 5	1, 2
2.	1, 2	4, 5
3.	1, 2	4, 5
4.	4, 5	1, 2
5.	1, 2	4, 5
6.	4, 5	1, 2

Quiz 7 — Sex

	Male	Female
1.	4, 5	1, 2
2.	1, 2	4, 5
3.	4, 5	1, 2
4.	1, 2	4, 5
5.	1, 2	4, 5
6.	4, 5	1, 2
7.	1, 2	4, 5
8.	1, 2	4, 5
9.	1, 2	4, 5
10.	4, 5	1, 2
11.	1, 2	4, 5
12.	4, 5	1, 2
13.	1, 2	4, 5

Quiz 8 — Home, Family, and Parenting

Section A — Parenting:

	Male	Female
1.	4, 5	1, 2
2.	4, 5	1, 2
3.	1, 2	4, 5
4.	4, 5	1, 2
5.	1, 2	4, 5
6.	4, 5	1, 2
7.	4, 5	1, 2
8.	1, 2	4, 5

Section B — Home and Family:

9.	4, 5	1, 2
10.	4, 5	1, 2
11.	4, 5	1, 2
12.	4, 5	1, 2
13.	1, 2	4, 5
14.	1, 2	4, 5
15.	1, 2	4, 5
16.	4, 5	1, 2
17.	1, 2	4, 5
18.	4, 5	1, 2
19.	1, 2	4, 5
20.	4, 5	1, 2
21.	4, 5	1, 2
22.	1, 2	4, 5

Quiz 9 — Hurting Each Other Often about Money or Power

	Male	Female
1.	1, 2	4, 5
2.	1, 2	4, 5
3.	1, 2	4, 5
4.	1, 2	4, 5
5.	1, 2	4, 5
6.	4, 5	1, 2
7.	4, 5	1, 2
8.	1, 2	4, 5
9.	4, 5	1, 2
10.	1, 2	4, 5
11.	4, 5	1, 2
12.	4, 5	1, 2
13.	4, 5	1, 2

About the Authors

Jeannette Lofas, CSW

Jeannette Lofas grew up between Europe and the United States, attending schools and universities on both sides of the Atlantic. Her family appeared in the social register both in Europe and the U.S. She grew up with the rituals of formal dinner parties and steamer ships to Europe, when passengers traveled with trunks full of formal gowns and matching shoes for each night of passage.

With her exceptional knowledge of languages and different cultures, she began an eighteen-year career as an international radio and television journalist, covering the news from Tokyo to Tangiers. She also worked as a film critic and an arts reporter for organizations such as Radio Free Europe, ABC-TV, and CBS-TV.

Married during the first part of her career, she had a son and was divorced after seven years. After another seven years as a single mother and an on-air television reporter, she remarried, left television, and moved to Aspen, Colorado.

Concerned about her stepfamily, she investigated and found little to no information. Faced with a problem she could not solve, Lofas let her journalistic instincts take charge. She co-authored the book *Living In Step — A Remarriage Manual* with Ruth Roosevelt, and was published in 1975 by Stein & Day. The book was republished as a quality paperback by McGraw Hill in 1978.

Living in Step was the first book ever to discuss the issues of family break up, stepfamilies, remarriage and children from all points of view. It was the first book to offer guidelines and solutions to the problems which now face over half the population. It remains in print and has sold over 60,000 copies.

At the same time, Lofas founded the Stepfamily Foundation, Inc., a not-for-profit organization which pioneered the study of how the stepfamily functions and does not function. The Stepfamily Foundation is recognized as the leading national organization in the field and has established innovative solution-oriented counseling techniques. It has established nationwide counseling services through its Counselor's Network.

In 1985 Lofas wrote *Stepparenting* (Zebra Books) and then created the audio book, *How to Be a Stepparent* in 1987 (Nightingale-Conant).

Lofas telephone counsels worldwide, lectures, and leads seminars to train and certify professionals. She continues to write, appear in the media, lecture worldwide, and counsel her clients on the characteristics of divorce, remarriage, and step relationships.

As she worked with couples since 1975, the issue of gender differences became more and more apparent. Now she also teaches clients and professionals how to work with, solve, and honor gender differences.

Lofas and MacMillan plan on forming another organization like the Stepfamily Foundation to inform, teach, and counsel about gender differences.

Joan MacMillan, MSC, MFCC

Growing up with first generation U.S. citizens from the midwest, Joan MacMillan's introduction to gender differences occurred during the days before women's liberation. Her mother served dinner the minute her father got home from work, and it was made clear that women did not work outside the home, drive cars, or get a college education. For the young MacMillan there was discomfort in the all too strict rituals of gender differences.

She knew that the messages she was receiving from her family weren't accurate and that her gender should not be a limiting factor. While she never officially joined the women's movement, she managed college with loans, scholarships, and part-time jobs. With her bachelor's degree, MacMillan began teaching family relations and child development in public schools. During her twenty-plus years in secondary and adult education which included teaching, counseling, staff development, and administration, she also earned a master of science degree in counseling.

As early as 1960, major gender differences became evident to MacMillan while working with her students: boys and girls seemed to approach almost everything differently, and they spoke different languages. The young teacher watched carefully, discovering that what she would later call "Malese" included a silent language and required different posturing, intonation, even thinking, She set about to become "bilingual." At one point, she was one of only ten women on a staff of sixty-five teachers and administrators and, without giving up her female self, she became part of both worlds.

After completing California's mandated 3000 hours of supervised internship and earning her Marriage, Family, Child Counselor license in 1982, MacMillan began her private practice featuring two specialties — hypnoanalysis and counseling with families, including work with the adolescent children. She is also the director of the west coast branch of the Stepfamily Foundation and the executive director of Carmichael Oaks Counseling Center, a complete counseling community of more than twenty therapists. Her clients' issues invariably include gender ignorance and injuries, and she is finding more and more that, as she includes gender literacy in her treatments, what once took many months of counseling has now become a shorter path to success.